Four F

Medea, Hippolytus, Heracles, Bacchae

by

Euripides

www.books.com.co

Published by LG Classics

First Printing March 2016
Printed in the United States of America.
10 9 8 7 6 5 4 3 2 1

LG Classics
New York, New York
www.books.com.co

TABLE OF CONTENTS

MEDEA

Dramatis Personae

NURSE OF MEDEA
ATTENDANT ON HER CHILDREN
MEDEA
CHORUS OF CORINTHIAN WOMEN
CREON, King of Corinth
JASON
AEGEUS, King of Athens
MESSENGER

Before MEDEA's house in Corinth, near the palace Of CREON. The NURSE enters from the house.

NURSE Ah! Would to Heaven the good ship Argo ne'er had sped its course to the Colchian land through the misty blue Symplegades, nor ever in the glens of Pelion the pine been felled to furnish with oars the chieftain's hands, who went to fetch the golden fleece for Pelias; for then would my own mistress Medea never have sailed to the turrets of Iolcos, her soul with love for Jason smitten, nor would she have beguiled the daughters of Pelias to slay their father and come to live here in the land of Corinth with her husband and children, where her exile found favour with the citizens to whose land she had come, and in all things of her own accord was she at one with Jason, the greatest safeguard this when wife and husband do agree; but now their love is all turned to hate, and tenderest ties are weak. For Jason hath betrayed his own children and my mistress dear for the love of a royal bride, for he hath wedded the daughter of Creon, lord of this land. While Medea, his hapless wife, thus scorned, appeals to the oaths he swore, recalls the strong pledge his right hand gave, and bids heaven be witness what requital she is finding from Jason. And here she lies fasting, yielding her body to her grief, wasting away in tears ever since she learnt that she was wronged by her husband, never lifting her eye nor raising her face from off the ground; and she lends as deaf an ear to her friend's warning as if she were a rock or ocean billow, save when she turns her snow-white neck aside and softly to herself bemoans her father dear, her country and her home, which she gave up to come hither with the man who now holds her in dishonour. She, poor lady, hath by sad experience learnt how good a thing it is never to quit one's native land. And she hates her children now and feels no joy at seeing them; I fear she may contrive some untoward scheme; for her mood is dangerous nor will she brook her cruel treatment; full well I know her, and I much do dread that she will plunge the keen sword through their hearts, stealing without a word into the chamber where their marriage couch is spread, or else that she will slay the prince and bridegroom too, and so find some calamity still more grievous than the present; for dreadful is her wrath; verily the man that doth incur her hate will have no easy task to raise o'er her a song of triumph. Lo! where her sons come hither from their childish sports; little they reck of their mother's woes, for the soul of the young is no friend to sorrow. (The ATTENDANT leads in MEDEA'S children.)

ATTENDANT Why dost thou, so long my lady's own handmaid, stand here at the gate alone, loudly lamenting to thyself the piteous tale? how comes it that Medea will have thee leave her to herself?

NURSE Old man, attendant on the sons of Jason, our masters' fortunes when they go awry make good slaves grieve and touch their hearts. Oh! have come to such a pitch of grief that there stole a yearning wish upon me to come forth hither and proclaim to heaven and earth my mistress's hard fate.

ATTENDANT What! has not the poor lady ceased yet

from her lamentation?

NURSE Would I were as thou art! the mischief is but now beginning; it has not reached its climax yet.

ATTENDANT O foolish one, if I may call my mistress such a name; how little she recks of evils yet more recent!

NURSE What mean'st, old man? grudge not to tell me.

ATTENDANT 'Tis naught; I do repent me even of the words I have spoken.

NURSE Nay, by thy beard I conjure thee, hide it not from thy fellow-slave; will be silent, if need be, on that text.

ATTENDANT I heard one say, pretending not to listen as I approached the place where our greybeards sit playing draughts near Pirene's sacred spring, that Creon, the ruler of this land, is bent on driving these children and their mother from the boundaries of Corinth; but I know not whether the news is to be relied upon, and would fain it were not.

NURSE What! will Jason brook such treatment of his sons, even though he be at variance with their mother?

ATTENDANT Old ties give way to new; he bears no longer any love to this family.

NURSE Undone, it seems, are we, if to old woes fresh ones we add, ere we have drained the former to the dregs.

ATTENDANT Hold thou thy peace, say not a word of this; 'tis no time for our mistress to learn hereof.

NURSE O children, do ye hear how your father feels towards you? Perdition catch him, but no he is my master still; yet is he proved a very traitor to his nearest and dearest.

ATTENDANT And who 'mongst men is not? Art learning only now, that every single man cares for himself more than for his neighbour, some from honest motives, others for mere gain's sake? seeing that to indulge his passion their father has ceased to love these children.

NURSE Go, children, within the house; all will be well. Do thou keep them as far away as may be, and bring them not near their mother in her evil hour. For ere this have I seen her eyeing them savagely, as though she were minded to do them some hurt, and well I know she will not cease from her fury till she have pounced on some victim. At least may she turn her hand against her foes, and not against her friends.

MEDEA (chanting within) Ah, me! a wretched suffering woman I! O would that I could die!

NURSE (chanting) 'Tis as I said, my dear children; wild fancies stir your mother's heart, wild fury goads her on. Into the house without delay, come not near her eye, approach her not, beware her savage mood, the fell tempest of her reckless heart. In, in with what speed ye may. For 'tis plain she will soon redouble her fury; that cry is but the herald of the gathering storm-cloud whose lightning soon will flash; what will her proud restless soul, in the anguish of despair, be guilty of? (The ATTENDANT takes the children into the house. MEDEA (chanting within) Ah, me! the agony I have suffered, deep enough to call for these laments! Curse you and your father too, ye children damned, sons of a doomed mother! Ruin seize the whole family!

NURSE (chanting) Ah me! ah me! the pity of it! Why, pray, do thy children share their father's crime? Why hatest thou them? Woe is you, poor children, how do I grieve for you lest ye suffer some outrage! Strange are the tempers of princes, and maybe because they seldom have to obey, and mostly lord it over others, change they their moods with difficulty. 'Tis better then to have been trained to live on equal terms. Be it mine to reach old age, not in proud pomp, but in security! Moderation wins the day first as a better word for men to use, and likewise it is far the best course for them to pursue; but greatness that doth o'erreach itself, brings no blessing to mortal men; but pays a penalty of greater ruin whenever fortune is wroth with a family. (The CHORUS enters. The following lines between the NURSE, CHORUS, and MEDEA are sung.)

CHORUS I heard the voice, uplifted loud, of our poor Colchian lady, nor yet is she quiet; speak, aged dame, for as I stood by the house with double gates I heard a voice of weeping from within, and I do grieve, lady, for the sorrows of this house, for it hath won my love.

NURSE 'Tis a house no more; all that is passed away long since; a royal bride keeps Jason at her side, while our mistress pines away in her bower, finding no comfort for her soul in aught her friends can say.

MEDEA (within) Oh, oh! Would that Heaven's levin bolt would cleave this head in twain! What gain is life to me? Woe, woe is me! O, to die and win release, quitting this loathed existence!

CHORUS Didst hear, O Zeus, thou earth, and thou, O light, the piteous note of woe the hapless wife is uttering? How shall a yearning for that insatiate resting-place ever hasten for thee, poor reckless one, the end that death alone can bring? Never pray for that. And if thy lord prefers a fresh love, be not angered with him for that; Zeus will judge 'twixt thee and him herein. Then mourn not for thy husband's loss too much, nor waste thyself away.

MEDEA (within) Great Themis, and husband of Themis, behold what I am suffering now, though I did bind that accursed one, my husband, by strong oaths to me! O, to see him and his bride some day brought to utter destruction, they and their house with them, for that they presume to wrong me thus unprovoked. O my father, my country, that I have left to my shame, after slaying my own brother.

NURSE Do ye hear her words, how loudly she adjures Themis, oft invoked, and Zeus, whom men regard as keeper of their oaths? On no mere trifle surely will our mistress spend her rage.

CHORUS Would that she would come forth for us to see, and listen to the words of counsel we might give, if haply she might lay aside the fierce fury of her wrath, and her temper stern. Never be my zeal at any rate denied my friends! But go thou and bring her hither outside the house, and tell her this our friendly thought; haste thee ere she do some mischief to those inside the house, for this sorrow of hers is mounting high.

NURSE This will I do; but I doubt whether I shall persuade my mistress; still willingly will I undertake this trouble for you; albeit, she glares upon her servants with the look of a lioness with cubs, whenso anyone draws nigh to speak to her. Wert thou to call the men of old time rude uncultured boors thou wouldst not err, seeing that they devised their hymns for festive occasions, for banquets, and to grace the board, a pleasure to catch the ear, shed o'er our life, but no man hath found a way to allay hated grief by music and the minstrel's varied strain, whence arise slaughters and fell strokes of fate to o'erthrow the homes of men. And yet this were surely a gain, to heal men's wounds by music's spell, but why tune they their idle song where rich banquets are spread? For of itself doth the rich banquet, set before them, afford to men delight.

CHORUS I heard a bitter cry of lamentation! loudly, bitterly she calls on the traitor of her marriage bed, her perfidious spouse; by grievous wrongs oppressed she invokes Themis, bride of Zeus, witness of oaths, who brought her unto Hellas, the land that fronts the strand of Asia, o'er the sea by night through ocean's boundless gate. (As the CHORUS finishes its song, MEDEA enters from the house.)

MEDEA From the house I have come forth, Corinthian ladies, for fear lest you be blaming me; for well I know that amongst men many by showing pride have gotten them an ill name and a reputation for indifference, both those who shun men's gaze and those who move amid the stranger crowd, and likewise they who choose a quiet walk in life. For there is no just discernment in the eyes of men, for they, or ever they have surely learnt their neighbour's heart, loathe him at first sight, though never wronged by him; and so a stranger most of all should adopt a city's views; nor do I commend that citizen, who, in the stubbornness of his heart, from churlishness resents the city's will.

But on me hath fallen this unforeseen disaster, and sapped my life; ruined I am, and long to resign the boon of existence, kind friends, and die. For he who was all the world to me, as well thou knowest, hath turned out the worst of men, my own husband. Of all things that have life and sense we women are the most hapless creatures; first must we buy a husband at a great price, and o'er ourselves a tyrant set which is an evil worse than the first; and herein lies the most important issue, whether our choice be good or bad. For divorce is not honourable to women, nor can we disown our lords. Next must the wife, coming as she does to ways and customs new, since she hath not learnt the lesson in her home, have a diviner's eye to see how best to treat the partner of her life. If haply we perform these tasks with thoroughness and tact, and the husband live with us, without resenting the yoke, our life is a happy one; if not, 'twere best to die. But when a man is vexed with what he finds indoors, he goeth forth and rids his soul of its disgust, betaking him to some friend or comrade of like age; whilst we must needs regard his single self.

And yet they say we live secure at home, while they are at the wars, with their sorry reasoning, for I would gladly take my stand in battle array three times o'er, than once give birth. But enough! this language suits not thee as it does me; thou hast a city here, a father's house, some joy in life, and friends to share thy thoughts, but I am destitute, without a city, and therefore scorned by my husband, a captive I from a foreign shore, with no mother, brother, or kinsman in whom to find a new haven of refuge from this calamity. Wherefore this one boon and only this I wish to win from thee,-thy silence, if haply I can some way or means devise to avenge me on my husband for this cruel treatment, and on the man who gave to him his daughter, and on her who is his wife. For though woman be timorous enough in all else, and as regards courage, a coward at the mere sight of steel, yet in the moment she finds her honour wronged, no heart is filled with deadlier thoughts than hers.

LEADER OF THE CHORUS This will I do; for thou wilt

be taking a just vengeance on thy husband, Medea. That thou shouldst mourn thy lot surprises me not. But lo! I see Creon, king of this land coming hither, to announce some new resolve. (CREON enters, with his retinue.)

CREON Hark thee, Medea, I bid thee take those sullen looks and angry thoughts against thy husband forth from this land in exile, and with thee take both thy children and that without delay, for I am judge in this sentence, and I will not return unto my house till I banish thee beyond the borders of the land.

MEDEA Ah, me! now is utter destruction come upon me, unhappy that I am! For my enemies are bearing down on me full sail, nor have I any landing-place to come at in my trouble. Yet for all my wretched plight I will ask thee, Creon, wherefore dost thou drive me from the land?

CREON I fear thee,-no longer need I veil my dread 'neath words,-lest thou devise against my child some cureless ill. Many things contribute to this fear of mine; thou art a witch by nature, expert in countless sorceries, and thou art chafing for the loss of thy husband's affection. I hear, too, so they tell me, that thou dost threaten the father of the bride, her husband, and herself with some mischief; wherefore I will take precautions ere our troubles come. For 'tis better for me to incur thy hatred now, lady, than to soften my heart and bitterly repent it hereafter.

MEDEA Alas! this is not now the first time, but oft before, O Creon, hath my reputation injured me and caused sore mischief. Wherefore whoso is wise in his generation ought never to have his children taught to be too clever; for besides the reputation they get for idleness, they purchase bitter odium from the citizens. For if thou shouldst import new learning amongst dullards, thou wilt be thought a useless trifler, void of knowledge; while if thy fame in the city o'ertops that of the pretenders to cunning knowledge, thou wilt win their dislike. I too myself share in this ill-luck. Some think me clever and hate me, others say I am too reserved, and some the very reverse; others find me hard to please and not so very clever after all. Be that as it may, thou dost fear me lest I bring on thee something to mar thy harmony. Fear me not, Creon, my position scarce is such that should seek to quarrel with princes. Why should I, for how hast thou injured me? Thou hast betrothed thy daughter where thy fancy prompted thee. No, ‘tis my husband I hate, though I doubt not thou hast acted wisely herein. And now I grudge not thy prosperity; betroth thy child, good luck to thee, but let me abide in this land, for though I have been wronged I will be still and yield to my superiors.

CREON Thy words are soft to hear, but much I dread lest thou art devising some mischief in thy heart, and less than ever do I trust thee now; for cunning woman, and man likewise, is easier to guard against when quick-tempered than when taciturn. Nay, begone at once! speak me no speeches, for this is decreed, nor hast thou any art whereby thou shalt abide amongst us, since thou hatest me.

MEDEA O, say not so! by thy knees and by thy daughter newlywed, I do implore!

CREON Thou wastest words; thou wilt never persuade me.

MEDEA What, wilt thou banish me, and to my prayers no pity yield?

CREON I will, for I love not thee above my own family.

MEDEA O my country! what fond memories I have of thee in this hour!

CREON Yea, for I myself love my city best of all things save my children.

MEDEA Ah me! ah me! to mortal man how dread a scourge is love!

CREON That, I deem, is according to the turn our fortunes take.

MEDEA O Zeus! let not the author of these my troubles

escape thee.

CREON Begone, thou silly woman, and free me from my toil.

MEDEA The toil is mine, no lack of it.

CREON Soon wilt thou be thrust out forcibly by the hand of servants.

MEDEA Not that, not that, I do entreat thee, Creon

CREON Thou wilt cause disturbance yet, it seems.

MEDEA I will begone; I ask thee not this boon to grant.

CREON Why then this violence? why dost thou not depart?

MEDEA Suffer me to abide this single day and devise some plan for the manner of my exile, and means of living for my children, since their father cares not to provide his babes therewith. Then pity them; thou too hast children of thine own; thou needs must have a kindly heart. For my own lot I care naught, though I an exile am, but for those babes I weep, that they should learn what sorrow means.

CREON Mine is a nature anything but harsh; full oft by showing pity have suffered shipwreck; and now albeit I clearly see my error, yet shalt thou gain this request, lady; but I do forewarn thee, if tomorrow's rising sun shall find thee and thy children within the borders of this land, thou diest; my word is spoken and it will not lie. So now, if abide thou must, stay this one day only, for in it thou canst not do any of the fearful deeds I dread. (CREON and his retinue go out.)

CHORUS (chanting) Ah! poor lady, woe is thee! Alas, for thy sorrows! Whither wilt thou turn? What protection, what home or country to save thee from thy troubles wilt thou find? O Medea, in what a hopeless sea of misery heaven hath plunged thee!

MEDEA On all sides sorrow pens me in. Who shall gainsay this? But all is not yet lost! think not so. Still are there troubles in store for the new bride, and for her bridegroom no light toil. Dost think I would ever have fawned on yonder man, unless to gain some end or form some scheme? Nay, would not so much as have spoken to him or touched him with my hand. But he has in folly so far stepped in that, though he might have checked my plot by banishing me from the land, he hath allowed me to abide this day, in which I will lay low in death three of my enemies-a father and his daughter and my husband too. Now, though I have many ways to compass their death, I am not sure, friends, which I am to try first. Shall I set fire to the bridal mansion, or plunge the whetted sword through their hearts, softly stealing into the chamber where their couch is spread? One thing stands in my way. If I am caught making my way into the chamber, intent on my design, I shall be put to death and cause my foes to mock, 'Twere best to take the shortest way-the way we women are most skilled in-by poison to destroy them. Well, suppose them dead; what city will receive me? What friendly host will give me a shelter in his land, a home secure, and save my soul alive? None. So I will wait yet a little while in case some tower of defence rise up for me; then will I proceed to this bloody deed in crafty silence; but if some unexpected mischance drive me forth, I will with mine own hand seize the sword, e'en though I die for it, and slay them, and go forth on my bold path of daring. By that dread queen whom I revere before all others and have chosen to share my task, by Hecate who dwells within my inmost chamber, not one of them shall wound my heart and rue it not. Bitter and sad will I make their marriage for them; bitter shall be the wooing of it, bitter my exile from the land. Up, then, Medea, spare not the secrets of thy art in plotting and devising; on to the danger. Now comes a struggle needing courage. Dost see what thou art suffering? 'Tis not for thee to be a laughing-stock to the race of Sisyphus by reason of this wedding of Jason, sprung, as thou art, from noble sire, and of the Sun-god's race. Thou hast cunning; and, more than this, we women, though by nature little apt for virtuous deeds, are most expert to fashion any mischief.

CHORUS (singing, strophe 1)

Back to their source the holy rivers turn their tide. Order and the universe are being reversed. 'Tis men whose counsels are treacherous, whose oath by heaven is no longer sure. Rumour shall bring a change o'er my life, bringing it into good repute. Honour's dawn is breaking for woman's sex; no more shall the foul tongue of slander fix upon us.

(antistrophe 1)

The songs of the poets of old shall cease to make our faithlessness their theme. Phoebus, lord of minstrelsy, hath not implanted in our mind the gift of heavenly song, else had I sung an answering strain to the race of males, for time's long chapter affords many a theme on their sex as well as ours.

(strophe 2)

With mind distraught didst thou thy father's house desert on thy voyage betwixt ocean's twin rocks, and on a foreign strand thou dwellest thy bed left husbandless, poor lady, and thou an exile from the land, dishonoured, persecuted.

(antistrophe 2)

Gone is the grace that oaths once had. Through all the breadth of Hellas honour is found no more; to heaven hath it sped away. For thee no father's house is open, woe is thee! to be a haven from the troublous storm, while o'er thy home is set another queen, the bride that is preferred to thee. (As the CHORUS finishes its song, JASON enters, alone. MEDEA comes out of the house.)

JASON It is not now I first remark, but oft ere this, how unruly a pest is a harsh temper. For instance, thou, hadst thou but patiently endured the will of thy superiors, mightest have remained here in this land and house, but now for thy idle words wilt thou be banished. Thy words are naught to me. Cease not to call Jason basest of men; but for those words thou hast spoken against our rulers, count it all gain that exile is thy only punishment. I ever tried to check the outbursts of the angry monarch, and would have had thee stay, but thou wouldst not forego thy silly rage, always reviling our rulers, and so thou wilt be banished. Yet even after all this I weary not of my goodwill, but am come with thus much forethought, lady, that thou mayst not be destitute nor want for aught, when, with thy sons, thou art cast out. Many an evil doth exile bring in its train with it; for even though thou hatest me, never will I harbour hard thoughts of thee.

MEDEA Thou craven villain (for that is the only name my tongue can find for thee, a foul reproach on thy unmanliness), comest thou to me, thou, most hated foe of gods, of me, and of all mankind? 'Tis no proof of courage or hardihood to confront thy friends after injuring them, but that worst of all human diseases-loss of shame. Yet hast thou done well to come; for I shall ease my soul by reviling thee, and thou wilt be vexed at my recital. I will begin at the very beginning. I saved thy life, as every Hellene knows who sailed with thee aboard the good ship Argo, when thou wert sent to tame and yoke fire-breathing bulls, and to sow the deadly tilth. Yea, and I slew the dragon which guarded the golden fleece, keeping sleepless watch o'er it with many a wreathed coil, and I raised for thee a beacon of deliverance. Father and home of my free will I left and came with the to Iolcos, 'neath Pelion's hills, for my love was stronger than my prudence. Next I caused the death of Pelias by a doom most grievous, even by his own children's hand, beguiling them of all their fear. All this have I done for thee, thou traitor! and thou hast cast me over, taking to thyself another wife, though children have been born to us. Hadst thou been childless still, I could have pardoned thy desire for this new union. Gone is now the trust I put in oaths. I cannot even understand whether thou thinkest that the gods of old no longer rule, or that fresh decrees are now in vogue amongst mankind, for thy conscience must tell thee thou hast not kept faith with me. Ah! poor right hand, which thou didst often grasp. These knees thou didst embrace! All in vain, I suffered a traitor to touch me! How short of my hopes I am fallen! But come, I will deal with the as though thou wert my friend. Yet what kindness can I expect from one so base as thee? But yet I will do it, for my questioning will show thee yet more base. Whither can I turn me now? to my father's house, to my own country, which I for thee deserted to come hither? to the hapless daughters of Pelias? A glad welcome, I trow, would they give me in their home, whose father's death I compassed! My case stands even thus: I am become the bitter foe to those of mine own home, and those whom I need ne'er have wronged I have made mine enemies to pleasure thee. Wherefore to reward me for this thou hast made me doubly blest in the eyes of many wife in Hellas; and in thee I own a peerless, trusty lord. O woe is me, if indeed I am to be cast forth an exile from the land, without one friend; one lone woman with her babes forlorn! Yea, a fine reproach to thee in thy bridal hour, that thy children and the wife who saved thy life are beggars and vagabonds! O Zeus! why hast thou granted unto man clear signs to know the sham in gold, while on man's brow no brand is stamped whereby to gauge the villain's heart?

LEADER OF THE CHORUS There is a something terrible and past all cure, when quarrels arise 'twixt those who are near and dear.

JASON Needs must I now, it seems, turn orator, and, like a good helmsman on a ship with close-reefed sails, weather that wearisome tongue of thine. Now, I believe, since thou wilt exaggerate thy favours, that to Cypri, alone of gods or men I owe the safety of my voyage. Thou hast a subtle wit enough; yet were it a hateful thing for me to say that the Love-god constrained thee by his resistless shaft to save my life. However, I will not reckon this too nicely; 'twas kindly done, however thou didst serve me. Yet for my safety hast thou received more than ever thou gavest, as I will show. First, thou dwellest in Hellas, instead of thy barbarian land, and hast learnt what justice means and how to live by law, not by the dictates of brute force; and all the Hellenes recognize thy cleverness, and thou hast gained a name; whereas, if thou hadst dwelt upon the confines of the earth, no tongue had mentioned thee. Give me no gold within my halls, nor skill to sing a fairer strain than ever Orpheus sang, unless there-with my fame be spread abroad! So much I say to thee about my own toils, for 'twas thou didst challenge me to this retort. As for the taunts thou urgest against my marriage with the princess, I will prove to thee, first, that I am prudent herein, next chastened in my love, and last powerful friend to thee and to thy sons; only hold thy peace. Since I have here withdrawn from Iolcos with many a hopeless trouble at my back, what happier device could I, an exile, frame than marriage with the daughter of the king? 'Tis not because I loathe thee for my wife-the thought that rankles in thy heart; 'tis not because I am smitten with desire for a new bride, nor yet that I am eager to vie with others in begetting many children, for those we have are quite enough, and I do not complain. Nay, 'tis that we-and this is most important-may dwell in comfort, instead of suffering want (for well I know that every whilom friend avoids the poor) , and that I might rear my sons as doth befit my house; further, that I might be the father of brothers for the children thou hast borne, and raise these to the same high rank, uniting the family in one,-to my lasting bliss. Thou, indeed, hast no need of more children, but me it profits to help my present family by that which is to be. Have I miscarried here? Not even thou wouldest say so unless a rival's charms rankled in thy bosom. No, but you women have such strange ideas, that you think all is well so long as your married life runs smooth; but if some mischance occur to ruffle your love, all that was good and lovely erst you reckon as your foes. Yea, men should have begotten children from some other source, no female race existing; thus would no evil ever have fallen on mankind.

LEADER This speech, O Jason, hast thou with specious art arranged; but yet I think-albeit in speaking I am indiscreet-that thou hast sinned in thy betrayal of thy wife.

MEDEA No doubt I differ from the mass of men on many points; for, to my mind, whoso hath skill to fence with words in an unjust cause, incurs the heaviest penalty; for such an one, confident that he can cast a decent veil of words o'er his injustice, dares to practise it; and yet he is not so very clever after all. So do not thou put forth thy specious pleas and clever words to me now, for one word of mine will lay thee low. Hadst thou not had a villain's heart, thou shouldst have gained my consent, then made this match, instead of hiding it from those who loved thee.

JASON Thou wouldest have lent me ready aid, no doubt, in this proposal, if had told thee of my marriage, seeing that not even now canst thou restrain thy soul's hot fury.

MEDEA This was not what restrained thee; but thine eye was turned towards old age, and a foreign wife began to appear a shame to thee.

JASON Be well assured of this: 'twas not for the woman's sake I wedded the king's daughter, my present wife; but, as I have already told thee, I wished to insure thy safety and to be the father of royal sons bound by blood to my own children-a bulwark to our house.

MEDEA May that prosperity, whose end is woe, ne'er be mine, nor such wealth as would ever sting my heart!

JASON Change that prayer as I will teach thee, and thou wilt show more wisdom. Never let happiness appear in sorrow's guise, nor, when thy fortune smiles, pretend she frowns!

MEDEA Mock on; thou hast a place of refuge; I am alone, an exile soon to be.

JASON Thy own free choice was this; blame no one else.

MEDEA What did I do? Marry, then betray thee?

JASON Against the king thou didst invoke an impious curse.

MEDEA On thy house too maybe I bring the curse.

JASON Know this, I will no further dispute this point with thee. But, if thou wilt of my fortune somewhat take for the children or thyself to help thy exile, say on; for I am ready to grant it with ungrudging hand, yea and to bend tokens to my friends elsewhere who shall treat thee well. If thou refuse this offer, thou wilt do a foolish deed, but if thou cease from anger the greater will be thy gain.

MEDEA I will have naught to do with friends of thine, naught will I receive of thee, offer it not to me; a villain's gifts can bring no blessing.

JASON At least I call the gods to witness, that I am ready in all things to serve thee and thy children, but thou dost scorn my favours and thrustest thy friends stubbornly away; wherefore thy lot will be more bitter still.

MEDEA Away! By love for thy young bride entrapped, too long thou lingerest outside her chamber; go wed, for, if God will, thou shalt have such a marriage as thou wouldst fain refuse. (JASON goes out.)

CHORUS (singing, strophe 1)

When in excess and past all limits Love doth come, he brings not glory or repute to man; but if the Cyprian queen in moderate might approach, no goddess is so full of charm as she. Never, O never, lady mine, discharge at me from thy golden bow a shaft invincible, in passion's venom dipped.

(antistrophe 1)

On me may chastity, heaven's fairest gift, look with a favouring eye; never may Cypris, goddess dread, fasten on me a temper to dispute, or restless jealousy, smiting my soul with mad desire for unlawful love, but may she hallow peaceful married life and shrewdly decide whom each of us shall wed.

(strophe 2)

O my country, O my own dear home! God grant I may never be an outcast from my city, leading that cruel helpless life, whose every day is misery. Ere that may I this life complete and yield to death, ay, death; for there is no misery that doth surpass the loss of fatherland.

(antistrophe 2)

I have seen with mine eyes, nor from the lips of others have I the lesson learnt; no city, not one friend doth pity thee in this thine awful woe. May he perish and find no favour, whoso hath not in him honour for his friends, freely unlocking his heart to them. Never shall he be friend of mine. (MEDEA has been seated in despair on her door-step during the choral song. AEGEUS and his attendants enter.)

AEGEUS All hail, Medea! no man knoweth fairer prelude to the greeting of friends than this.

MEDEA All hail to thee likewise, Aegeus, son of wise Pandion. Whence comest thou to this land?

AEGEUS From Phoebus' ancient oracle.

MEDEA What took thee on thy travels to the prophetic centre of the earth?

AEGEUS The wish to ask how I might raise up seed unto myself.

MEDEA Pray tell me, hast thou till now dragged on a childless life?

AEGEUS I have no child owing to the visitation of some god.

MEDEA Hast thou a wife, or hast thou never known the married state?

AEGEUS I have a wife joined to me in wedlock's bond.

MEDEA What said Phoebus to thee as to children?

AEGEUS Words too subtle for man to comprehend.

MEDEA Surely I may learn the god's answer?

AEGEUS Most assuredly, for it is just thy subtle wit it needs.

MEDEA What said the god? speak, if I may hear it.

AEGEUS He bade me "not loose the wineskin's pendent neck."

MEDEA Till when? what must thou do first, what country visit?

AEGEUS Till I to my native home return.

MEDEA What object hast thou in sailing to this land?

AEGEUS O'er Troezen's realm is Pittheus king.

MEDEA Pelops' son, a man devout they say.

AEGEUS To him I fain would impart the oracle of the god.

MEDEA The man is shrewd and versed in such-like lore.

AEGEUS Aye, and to me the dearest of all my warrior friends.

MEDEA Good luck to thee! success to all thy wishes!

AEGEUS But why that downcast eye, that wasted cheek?

MEDEA O Aegeus, my husband has proved most evil.

AEGEUS What meanest thou? explain to me clearly the cause of thy despondency.

MEDEA Jason is wronging me though I have given him no cause.

AEGEUS What hath he done? tell me more clearly.

MEDEA He is taking another wife to succeed me as mistress of his house.

AEGEUS Can he have brought himself to such a dastard deed?

MEDEA Be assured thereof; I, whom he loved of yore, am in dishonour now.

AEGEUS Hath he found a new love? or does he loathe thy bed?

MEDEA Much in love is he! A traitor to his friend is he

become.

AEGEUS Enough! if he is a villain as thou sayest.

MEDEA The alliance he is so much enamoured of is with a princess.

AEGEUS Who gives his daughter to him? go on, I pray.

MEDEA Creon, who is lord of this land of Corinth.

AEGEUS Lady, I can well pardon thy grief.

MEDEA I am undone, and more than that, am banished from the land.

AEGEUS By whom? fresh woe this word of thine unfolds.

MEDEA Creon drives me forth in exile from Corinth.

AEGEUS Doth Jason allow it? This too I blame him for.

MEDEA Not in words, but he will not stand out against it. O, I implore thee by this beard and by thy knees, in suppliant posture, pity, O pity my sorrows; do not see me cast forth forlorn, but receive me in thy country, to a seat within thy halls. So may thy wish by heaven's grace be crowned with a full harvest of offspring, and may thy life close in happiness! Thou knowest not the rare good luck thou findest here, for I will make thy childlessness to cease and cause thee to beget fair issue; so potent are the spells I know.

AEGEUS Lady, on many grounds I am most fain to grant thee this thy boon, first for the gods' sake, next for the children whom thou dost promise I shall beget; for in respect of this I am completely lost. 'Tis thus with me; if e'er thou reach my land, I will attempt to champion thee as I am bound to do. Only one warning I do give thee first, lady; I will not from this land bear thee away, yet if of thyself thou reach my halls, there shalt thou bide in safety and I will never yield thee up to any man. But from this land escape without my aid, for I have no wish to incur the blame of my allies as well.

MEDEA It shall be even so; but wouldst thou pledge thy word to this, I should in all be well content with thee.

AEGEUS Surely thou dost trust me? or is there aught that troubles thee?

MEDEA Thee I trust; but Pelias' house and Creon are my foes. Wherefore, if thou art bound by an oath, thou wilt not give me up to them when they come to drag me from the land, but, having entered into a compact and sworn by heaven as well, thou wilt become my friend and disregard their overtures. Weak is any aid of mine, whilst they have wealth and a princely house.

AEGEUS Lady, thy words show much foresight, so if this is thy will, I do not, refuse. For I shall feel secure and safe if I have some pretext to offer to thy foes, and thy case too the firmer stands. Now name thy gods.

MEDEA Swear by the plain of Earth, by Helios my father's sire, and, in one comprehensive oath, by all the race of gods.

AEGEUS What shall I swear to do, from what refrain? tell me that.

MEDEA Swear that thou wilt never of thyself expel me from thy land, nor, whilst life is thine, permit any other, one of my foes maybe, to hale me thence if so he will.

AEGEUS By Earth I swear, by the Sun-god's holy beam and by all the host of heaven that I will stand fast to the terms I hear thee make.

MEDEA 'Tis enough. If thou shouldst break this oath, what curse dost thou invoke upon thyself?

AEGEUS Whate'er betides the impious.

MEDEA Go in peace; all is well, and I with what speed I may, will to thy city come, when I have wrought my purpose and obtained my wish. (AEGEUS and his retinue depart.)

CHORUS (chanting) May Maia's princely son go with

thee on thy way to bring thee to thy home, and mayest thou attain that on which thy soul is set so firmly, for to my mind thou seemest a generous man, O Aegeus.

MEDEA O Zeus, and Justice, child of Zeus, and Sun-god's light, now will triumph o'er my foes, kind friends; on victory's road have I set forth; good hope have I of wreaking vengeance on those I hate. For where we were in most distress this stranger hath appeared, to be a haven in my counsels; to him will we make fast the cables of our ship when we come to the town and citadel of Pallas. But now will I explain to thee my plans in full; do not expect to hear a pleasant tale. A servant of mine will I to Jason send and crave an interview; then when he comes I will address him with soft words, say, "this pleases me," and, "that is well," even the marriage with the princess, which my treacherous lord is celebrating, and add "it suits us both, 'twas well thought out"; then will I entreat that here my children may abide, not that I mean to leave them in a hostile land for foes to flout, but that I may slay the king's daughter by guile. For I will send them with gifts in their hands, carrying them unto the bride to save them from banishment, a robe of finest woof and a chaplet of gold. And if these ornaments she take and put them on, miserably shall she die, and likewise everyone who touches her; with such fell poisons will I smear my gifts. And here I quit this theme; but I shudder at the deed I must do next; for I will slay the children I have borne; there is none shall take them from my toils; and when I have utterly confounded Jason's house I will leave the land, escaping punishment for my dear children's murder, after my most unholy deed. For I cannot endure the taunts of enemies, kind friends; enough! what gain is life to me? I have no country, home, or refuge left. O, I did wrong, that hour I left my father's home, persuaded by that Hellene's words, who now shall pay the penalty, so help me God, Never shall he see again alive the children I bore to him, nor from his new bride shall he beget issue, for she must die a hideous death, slain by my drugs. Let no one deem me a poor weak woman who sits with folded hands, but of another mould, dangerous to foes and well-disposed to friends; for they win the fairest fame who live then, life like me.

LEADER OF THE CHORUS Since thou hast imparted this design to me, I bid thee hold thy hand, both from a wish to serve thee and because I would uphold the laws men make.

MEDEA It cannot but be so; thy words I pardon since thou art not in the same sorry plight that I am.

LEADER O lady, wilt thou steel thyself to slay thy children twain?

MEDEA I will, for that will stab my husband to the heart.

LEADER It may, but thou wilt be the saddest wife alive.

MEDEA No matter; wasted is every word that comes 'twixt now and then. Ho! (The NURSE enters in answer to her call.) Thou, go call me Jason hither, for thee I do employ on every mission of trust. No word divulge of all my purpose, as thou art to thy mistress loyal and likewise of my sex. (The NURSE goes out.)

CHORUS (singing, strophe 1)

Sons of Erechtheus, heroes happy from of yore, children of the blessed gods, fed on wisdom's glorious food in a holy land ne'er pillaged by its foes, ye who move with sprightly step through a climate ever bright and clear, where, as legend tells, the Muses nine, Pieria's holy maids, were brought to birth by Harmonia with the golden hair.

(antistrophe 1)

And poets sing how Cypris drawing water from the streams of fair-flowing Cephissus breathes o'er the land a gentle breeze of balmy winds, and ever as she crowns her tresses with a garland of sweet rose-buds sends forth the Loves to sit by wisdom's side, to take part in every excellence.

(strophe 2)

How then shall the city of sacred streams, the land that

welcomes those it loves, receive thee, the murderess of thy children, thee whose presence with others is a pollution? 'Think on the murder of thy children, consider the bloody deed thou takest on thee. Nay, by thy knees we, one and all, implore thee, slay not thy babes.

(antistrophe 2)

Where shall hand or heart find hardihood enough in wreaking such a fearsome deed upon thy sons? How wilt thou look upon thy babes, and still without a tear retain thy bloody purpose? Thou canst not, when they fall at thy feet for mercy, steel thy heart and dip in their blood thy hand. (JASON enters.)

JASON I am come at thy bidding, for e'en though thy hate for me is bitter thou shalt not fail in this small boon, but I will hear what new request thou hast to make of me, lady.

MEDEA Jason, I crave thy pardon for the words I spoke, and well thou mayest brook my burst of passion, for ere now we twain have shared much love. For I have reasoned with my soul and railed upon me thus, "Ah! poor heart! why am I thus distraught, why so angered 'gainst all good advice, why have I come to hate the rulers of the land, my husband too, who does the best for me he can, in wedding with a princess and rearing for my children noble brothers? Shall I not cease to fret? What possesses me, when heaven its best doth offer? Have I not my children to consider? do I forget that we are fugitives, in need of friends?" When I had thought all this I saw how foolish I had been, how senselessly enraged. So now do commend thee and think thee most wise in forming this connection for us; but I was mad, I who should have shared in these designs, helped on thy plans, and lent my aid to bring about the match, only too pleased to wait upon thy bride. But what we are, we are, we women, evil I will not say; wherefore thou shouldst not sink to our sorry level nor with our weapons meet our childishness.

I yield and do confess that I was wrong then, but now have I come to a better mind. Come hither, my children, come, leave the house, step forth, and with me greet and bid farewell to your father, be reconciled from all past bitterness unto your friends, as now your mother is; for we have made a truce and anger is no more. (The ATTENDANT comes out of the house with the children.) Take his right hand; ah me! my sad fate! when I reflect, as now, upon the hidden future. O my children, since there awaits you even thus a long, long life, stretch forth the hand to take a fond farewell. Ah me! how new to tears am I, how full of fear! For now that I have at last released me from my quarrel with your father, I let the tear-drops stream adown my tender cheek.

LEADER OF THE CHORUS From my eyes too bursts forth the copious tear; O, may no greater ill than the present e'er befall!

JASON Lady, I praise this conduct, not that I blame what is past; for it is but natural to the female sex to vent their spleen against a husband when he trafficks in other marriages besides his own. But thy heart is changed to wiser schemes and thou art determined on the better course, late though it be; this is acting like a woman of sober sense. And for you, my sons, hath your father provided with all good heed a sure refuge, by God's grace; for ye, I trow, shall with your brothers share hereafter the foremost rank in this Corinthian realm. Only grow up, for all the rest your sire and whoso of the gods is kind to us is bringing to pass. May I see you reach man's full estate, high o'er the heads of those I hate! But thou, lady, why with fresh tears dost thou thine eyelids wet, turning away thy wan cheek, with no welcome for these my happy tidings?

MEDEA 'Tis naught; upon these children my thoughts were turned.

JASON Then take heart; for I will see that it is well with them.

MEDEA I will do so; nor will I doubt thy word; woman is a weak creature, ever given to tears.

JASON Why prithee, unhappy one, dost moan o'er these

children?

MEDEA I gave them birth; and when thou didst pray long life for them, pity entered into my soul to think that these things must be. But the reason of thy coming hither to speak with me is partly told, the rest will I now mention. Since it is the pleasure of the rulers of the land to banish me, and well I know 'twere best for me to stand not in the way of thee or of the rulers by dwelling here, enemy as I am thought unto their house, forth from this land in exile am I going, but these children,-that they may know thy fostering hand, beg Creon to remit their banishment.

JASON I doubt whether I can persuade him, yet must I attempt it.

MEDEA At least do thou bid thy wife ask her sire this boon, to remit the exile of the children from this land.

JASON Yea, that will I; and her methinks I shall persuade, since she is woman like the rest.

MEDEA I too will aid thee in this task, for by the children's hand I will send to her gifts that far surpass in beauty, I well know, aught that now is seen 'mongst men, a robe of finest tissue and a chaplet of chased gold. But one of my attendants must haste and bring the ornaments hither. (A servant goes into the house.) Happy shall she be not once alone but ten thousand-fold, for in thee she wins the noblest soul to share her love, and gets these gifts as well which on a day my father's sire, the Sun-god, bestowed on his descendants. (The servant returns and hands the gifts to the children.) My children, take in your hands these wedding gifts, and bear them as an offering to the royal maid, the happy bride; for verily the gifts she shall receive are not to be scorned.

JASON But why so rashly rob thyself of these gifts? Dost think a royal palace wants for robes or gold? Keep them, nor give them to another. For well I know that if my lady hold me in esteem, she will set my price above all wealth.

MEDEA Say not so; 'tis said that gifts tempt even gods;

and o'er men's minds gold holds more potent sway than countless words. Fortune smiles upon thy bride, and heaven now doth swell her triumph; youth is hers and princely power; yet to save my children from exile I would barter life, not dross alone. Children, when we are come to the rich palace, pray your father's new bride, my mistress, with suppliant voice to save you from exile, offering her these ornaments the while; for it is most needful that she receive the gifts in her own hand. Now go and linger not; may ye succeed and to your mother bring back the glad tidings she fain would hear (JASON, the ATTENDANT, and the children go out together.)

CHORUS (singing, strophe 1)

Gone, gone is every hope I had that the children yet might live; forth to their doom they now proceed. The hapless bride will take, ay, take the golden crown that is to be her ruin; with her own hand will she lift and place upon her golden locks the garniture of death.

(antistrophe 1)

Its grace and sheen divine will tempt her to put on the robe and crown of gold, and in that act will she deck herself to be a bride amid the dead. Such is the snare whereinto she will fall, such is the deadly doom that waits the hapless maid, nor shall she from the curse escape.

(strophe 2)

And thou, poor wretch, who to thy sorrow art wedding a king's daughter, little thinkest of the doom thou art bringing on thy children's life, or of the cruel death that waits thy bride. Woe is thee! how art thou fallen from thy high estate!

(antistrophe 2)

Next do I bewail thy sorrows, O mother hapless in thy children, thou who wilt slay thy babes because thou hast a rival, the babes thy husband hath deserted impiously to join him to another bride. (The ATTENDANT enters with the children.)

ATTENDANT Thy children, lady, are from exile freed, and gladly did the royal bride accept thy gifts in her own hands, and so thy children made their peace with her.

MEDEA Ah!

ATTENDANT Why art so disquieted in thy prosperous hour? Why turnest thou thy cheek away, and hast no welcome for my glad news?

MEDEA Ah me!

ATTENDANT These groans but ill accord with the news I bring.

MEDEA Ah me! once more I say.

ATTENDANT Have I unwittingly announced some evil tidings? Have I erred in thinking my news was good?

MEDEA Thy news is as it is; I blame thee not.

ATTENDANT Then why this downcast eye, these floods of tears?

MEDEA Old friend, needs must I weep; for the gods and I with fell intent devised these schemes.

ATTENDANT Be of good cheer; thou too of a surety shalt by thy sons yet be brought home again.

MEDEA Ere that shall I bring others to their home, ah! woe is me

ATTENDANT Thou art not the only mother from thy children reft. Bear patiently thy troubles as a mortal must.

MEDEA I will obey; go thou within the house and make the day's provision for the children. (The ATTENDANT enters the house. MEDEA turns to the children.) O my babes, my babes, ye have still a city and a home, where far from me and my sad lot you will live your lives, reft of your mother for ever; while I must to another land in banishment, or ever I have had my joy of you, or lived to see you happy, or ever I have graced your marriage couch, your bride, your bridal bower, or lifted high the wedding torch. Ah me! a victim of my own self-will. So it was all in vain I reared you, O my sons; in vain did suffer, racked with anguish, enduring the cruel pangs of childbirth. 'Fore Heaven I once had hope, poor me! high hope of ye that you would nurse me in my age and deck my corpse with loving hands, a boon we mortals covet; but now is my sweet fancy dead and gone; for I must lose you both and in bitterness and sorrow drag through life. And ye shall never with fond eyes see your mother more for o'er your life there comes a change. Ah me! ah me! why do ye look at me so, my children? why smile that last sweet smile? Ah me! what am I to do? My heart gives way when I behold my children's laughing eyes. O, I cannot; farewell to all my former schemes; I will take the children from the land, the babes I bore. Why should I wound their sire by wounding them, and get me a twofold measure of sorrow? No, no, I will not do it. Farewell my scheming! And yet what possesses me? Can I consent to let those foes of mine escape from punishment, and incur their mockery? I must face this deed. Out upon my craven heart! to think that I should even have let the soft words escape my soul. Into the house, children! (The children go into the house.) And whoso feels he must not be present at my sacrifice, must see to it himself; I will not spoil my handiwork. Ah! ah! do not, my heart, O do not do this deed! Let the children go, unhappy one, spare the babes! For if they live, they will cheer thee in our exile there. Nay, by the fiends of hell's abyss, never, never will I hand my children over to their foes to mock and flout. Die they must in any case, and since 'tis so, why I, the mother who bore them, will give the fatal blow. In any case their doom is fixed and there is no escape. Already the crown is on her head, the robe is round her, and she is dying, the royal bride; that do I know full well. But now since I have a piteous path to tread, and yet more piteous still the path I send my children on, fain would I say farewell to them. (The children come out at her call. She takes them in her arms.) O my babes, my babes, let your mother kiss your hands. Ah! hands I love so well, O lips most dear to me! O noble form and features of my children, I wish ye joy, but in that other land, for here your father robs you of your home. O the sweet embrace, the soft young cheek, the fragrant breath! my children! Go, leave me; I cannot bear to longer look upon ye; my sorrow wins the day. At last I understand the awful deed I am to do; but passion, that cause of direst woes to mortal man, hath triumphed o'er my sober thoughts. (She goes into the house with the children.)

CHORUS (chanting) Oft ere now have I pursued subtler themes and have faced graver issues than woman's sex should seek to probe; but then e'en we aspire to culture, which dwells with us to teach us wisdom; I say not all; for small is the class amongst women-(one maybe shalt thou find 'mid many)-that is not incapable of wisdom. And amongst mortals I do assert that they who are wholly without experience and have never had children far surpass in happiness those who are parents. The childless, because they have never proved whether children grow up to be a blessing or curse to men are removed from all share in many troubles; whilst those who have a sweet race of children growing up in their houses do wear away, as I perceive, their whole life through; first with the thought how they may train them up in virtue, next how they shall leave their sons the means to live; and after all this 'tis far from clear whether on good or bad children they bestow their toil. But one last crowning woe for every mortal man now will name; suppose that they have found sufficient means to live, and seen their children grow to man's estate and walk in virtue's path, still if fortune so befall, comes Death and bears the children's bodies off to Hades. Can it be any profit to the gods to heap upon us mortal men beside our other woes this further grief for children lost, a grief surpassing all? (MEDEA comes out of the house.)

MEDEA Kind friends, long have I waited expectantly to know how things would at the palace chance. And lo! I see one of Jason's servants coming hither, whose hurried gasps for breath proclaim him the bearer of some fresh tidings. (A MESSENGER rushes in.)

MESSENGER Fly, fly, Medea! who hast wrought an awful deed, transgressing every law: nor leave behind or seaborne bark or car that scours the plain.

MEDEA Why, what hath chanced that calls for such a flight of mine?

MESSENGER The princess is dead, a moment gone, and Creon too, her sire, slain by those drugs of thine.

MEDEA Tidings most fair are thine! Henceforth shalt thou be ranked amongst my friends and benefactors.

MESSENGER Ha! What? Art sane? Art not distraught, lady, who hearest with joy the outrage to our royal house done, and art not at the horrid tale afraid?

MEDEA Somewhat have I, too, to say in answer to thy words. Be not so hasty, friend, but tell the manner of their death, for thou wouldst give me double joy, if so they perished miserably.

MESSENGER When the children twain whom thou didst bear came with their father and entered the palace of the bride, right glad were we thralls who had shared thy griefs, for instantly from ear to ear a rumour spread that thou and thy lord had made up your former quarrel. One kissed thy children's hands, another their golden hair, while I for very joy went with them in person to the women's chambers. Our mistress, whom now we do revere in thy room, cast a longing glance at Jason, ere she saw thy children twain; but then she veiled her eyes and turned her blanching cheek away, disgusted at their coming; but thy husband tried to check his young bride's angry humour with these words: "O, be not angered 'gainst thy friends; cease from wrath and turn once more thy face this way, counting as friends whomso thy husband counts, and accept these gifts, and for my sake crave thy sire to remit these children's exile." Soon as she saw the ornaments, no longer she held out, but yielded to her lord in all; and ere the father and his sons were far from the palace gone, she took the broidered robe and put it on, and set the golden crown about her tresses, arranging her hair at her bright mirror, with many a happy smile at her breathless counterfeit. Then rising from her seat she passed across the chamber, tripping lightly on her fair white foot, exulting in the gift, with many a glance at her uplifted ankle. When lo! a scene of awful horror did ensue. In a moment she turned pale, reeled backwards, trembling in every limb, and sinks upon a seat scarce soon enough to save herself from falling to the ground. An aged dame, one of her company, thinking belike it was a fit from Pan or some god sent, raised a cry of prayer, till from her mouth she saw the foam-flakes issue, her eyeballs rolling in their sockets, and all the blood her face desert; then did she raise a loud scream far different from her former cry. Forthwith one handmaid rushed to her father's house, another to her new bridegroom to tell his bride's sad fate, and the whole house echoed with their running to and fro. By this time would a quick walker have made the turn in a course of six plethra and reached the goal, when she with one awful shriek awoke, poor sufferer, from her speechless trance and oped her closed eyes, for against her a twofold anguish was warring. The chaplet of gold about her head was sending forth a wondrous stream of ravening flame, while the fine raiment, thy children's gift, was preying on the hapless maiden's fair white flesh; and she starts from her seat in a blaze and seeks to fly, shaking her hair and head this way and that, to cast the crown therefrom; but the gold held firm to its fastenings, and the flame, as she shook her locks, blazed forth the more with double fury. Then to the earth she sinks, by the cruel blow o'ercome; past all recognition now save to a father's eye; for her eyes had lost their tranquil gaze, her face no more its natural look preserved, and from the crown of her head blood and fire in mingled stream ran down; and from her bones the flesh kept peeling off beneath the gnawing of those secret drugs, e'en as when the pine-tree weeps its tears of pitch, a fearsome sight to see. And all were afraid to touch the corpse, for we were warned by what had chanced. Anon came her haples father unto the house, all unwitting of her doom, and stumbles o'er the dead, and loud he cried, and folding his arms about her kissed her, with words like these the while, "O my poor, poor child, which of the gods hath destroyed thee thus foully? Who is robbing me of thee, old as I am and ripe for death? O my child, alas! would I could die with thee!" He ceased his sad lament, and would have raised his aged frame, but found himself held fast by the fine-spun robe as ivy that clings to the branches of the bay, and then ensued a fearful struggle. He strove to rise, but she still held him back; and if ever he pulled with all his might, from off his bones his aged flesh he tore. At last he gave it up, and breathed forth his soul in awful suffering; for he could no longer master the pain. So there they lie, daughter and aged sire, dead side by side, a grievous sight that calls for tears. And as for thee, I leave thee out of my consideration, for thyself must discover a means to escape punishment. Not now for the first time I think this human life a shadow; yea, and without shrinking I will say that they amongst men who pretend to wisdom and expend deep thought on words do incur a serious charge of folly; for amongst mortals no man is happy; wealth may pour in and make one luckier than another, but none can happy be. (The MESSENGER departs.)

LEADER OF THE CHORUS This day the deity, it seems, will mass on Jason, as he well deserves, heavy load of evils. Woe is thee, daughter of Creon We pity thy sad fate, gone as thou art to Hades' halls as the price of thy marriage with Jason.

MEDEA My friends, I am resolved upon the deed; at once will I slay my children and then leave this land, without delaying long enough to hand them over to some more savage hand to butcher. Needs must they die in any case; and since they must, I will slay them-I, the mother that bare them. O heart of mine, steel thyself! Why do I hesitate to do the awful deed that must be done? Come, take the sword, thou wretched hand of mine! Take it, and advance to the post whence starts thy life of sorrow! Away with cowardice! Give not one thought to thy babes, how dear they are or how thou art their mother. This one brief day forget thy children dear, and after that lament; for though thou wilt slay them yet they were thy darlings still, and I am a lady of sorrows. (MEDEA enters the house.)

CHORUS (chanting) O earth, O sun whose beam illumines all, look, look upon this lost woman, ere she stretch forth her murderous hand upon her sons for blood; for lo! these are scions of thy own golden seed, and the blood of gods is in danger of being shed by man. O light, from Zeus proceeding, stay her, hold her hand, forth from the house chase this fell bloody fiend by demons led. Vainly wasted were the throes thy children cost thee; vainly hast thou borne, it seems, sweet babes, O thou who hast left behind thee that passage through the blue Symplegades, that strangers justly hate. Ah! hapless one, why doth fierce anger thy soul assail? Why in its place is fell murder growing up? For grievous unto mortal men are pollutions that come of kindred blood poured on the earth, woes to suit each crime hurled from heaven on the murderer's house.

FIRST SON (within) Ah, me; what can I do? Whither fly to escape my mother's blows?

SECOND SON (within) I know not, sweet brother mine; we are lost.

CHORUS (chanting) Didst hear, didst hear the children's cry? O lady, born to sorrow, victim of an evil fate! Shall I enter the house? For the children's sake I am resolved to ward off the murder.

FIRST SON (within) Yea, by heaven I adjure you; help, your aid is needed.

SECOND SON (within) Even now the toils of the sword are closing round us.

CHORUS (chanting) O hapless mother, surely thou hast a heart of stone or steel to slay the offspring of thy womb by such a murderous doom. Of all the wives of yore I know but one who laid her hand upon her children dear, even Ino, whom the gods did madden in the day that the wife of Zeus drove her wandering from her home. But she, poor sufferer, flung herself into the sea because of the foul murder of her children, leaping o'er the wave-beat cliff, and in her death was she united to her children twain. Can there be any deed of horror left to follow this? Woe for the wooing of women fraught with disaster! What sorrows hast thou caused for men ere now! (JASON and his attendants enter.)

JASON Ladies, stationed near this house, pray tell me is the author of these hideous deeds, Medea, still within, or hath she fled from hence? For she must hide beneath the earth or soar on wings towards heaven's vault, if she would avoid the vengeance of the royal house. Is she so sure she will escape herself unpunished from this house, when she hath slain the rulers of the land? But enough of this! I am forgetting her children. As for her, those whom she hath wronged will do the like by her; but I am come to save the children's life, lest the victim's kin visit their wrath on me, in vengeance for the murder foul, wrought by my children's mother.

LEADER OF THE CHORUS Unhappy man, thou knowest not the full extent of thy misery, else had thou never said those words.

JASON How now? Can she want to kill me too?

LEADER Thy sons are dead; slain by their own mother's hand.

JASON O God! what sayest thou? Woman, thou hast sealed my doom.

LEADER Thy children are no more; be sure of this.

JASON Where slew she them; within the palace or outside?

LEADER Throw wide the doors and see thy children's murdered corpses.

JASON Haste, ye slaves, loose the bolts, undo the fastenings, that I may see the sight of twofold woe, my murdered sons and her, whose blood in vengeance I will shed. (MEDEA appears above the house, on a chariot drawn by dragons; the children's corpses are beside her.)

MEDEA Why shake those doors and attempt to loose their bolts, in quest of the dead and me their murderess? From such toil desist. If thou wouldst aught with me, say on, if so thou wilt; but never shalt thou lay hand on me, so swift the steeds the sun, my father's sire, to me doth give to save me from the hand of my foes.

JASON Accursed woman! by gods, by me and all mankind abhorred as never woman was, who hadst the heart to stab thy babes, thou their mother, leaving me undone and childless; this hast thou done and still dost gaze upon the sun and earth after this deed most impious. Curses on thee! now perceive what then I missed in the day I brought thee, fraught with doom, from thy home in a barbarian land to dwell in Hellas, traitress to thy sire and to the land that nurtured thee. On me the gods have hurled the curse that dogged thy steps, for thou didst slay thy brother at his hearth ere thou cam'st aboard our fair ship, Argo. Such was the outset of thy life of crime; then didst thou wed with me, and having borne me sons to glut thy passion's lust, thou now hast slain them. Not one amongst the wives of Hellas e'er had dared this deed; yet before them all I chose thee for my wife, wedding a foe to be my doom, no woman, but a lioness fiercer than Tyrrhene Scylla in nature. But with reproaches heaped thousandfold I cannot wound thee, so brazen is thy nature. Perish, vile sorceress, murderess of thy babes! Whilst I must mourn my luckless fate, for I shall ne'er enjoy my new-found bride, nor shall I have the children, whom I bred and reared, alive to say the last farewell to me; nay, I have lost them.

MEDEA To this thy speech I could have made a long reply, but Father Zeus knows well all I have done for thee, and the treatment thou hast given me. Yet thou wert not ordained to scorn my love and lead a life of joy in mockery of me, nor was thy royal bride nor Creon, who gave thee a second wife, to thrust me from this land and rue it not. Wherefore, if thou wilt, call me e'en a lioness, and Scylla, whose home is in the Tyrrhene land; for I in turn have wrung thy heart, as well I might.

JASON Thou, too, art grieved thyself, and sharest in my sorrow.

MEDEA Be well assured I am; but it relieves my pain to

know thou canst not mock at me.

JASON O my children, how vile a mother ye have found!

MEDEA My sons, your father's feeble lust has been your ruin!

JASON 'Twas not my hand, at any rate, that slew them.

MEDEA No, but thy foul treatment of me, and thy new marriage.

JASON Didst think that marriage cause enough to murder them?

MEDEA Dost think a woman counts this a trifling injury?

JASON So she be self-restrained; but in thy eyes all is evil.

MEDEA Thy sons are dead and gone. That will stab thy heart.

JASON They live, methinks, to bring a curse upon thy head.

MEDEA The gods know, whoso of them began this troublous coil.

JASON Indeed, they know that hateful heart of thine.

MEDEA Thou art as hateful. I am aweary of thy bitter tongue.

JASON And I likewise of thine. But parting is easy.

MEDEA Say how; what am I to do? for I am fain as thou to go.

JASON Give up to me those dead, to bury and lament.

MEDEA No, never! I will bury them myself, bearing them to Hera's sacred field, who watches o'er the Cape, that none of their foes may insult them by pulling down their tombs; and in this land of Sisyphus I will ordain hereafter a solemn feast and mystic rites to atone for this impious murder. Myself will now to the land of Erechtheus, to dwell with Aegeus, Pandion's son. But thou, as well thou mayst, shalt die a caitiff's death, thy head crushed 'neath a shattered relic of Argo, when thou hast seen the bitter ending of my marriage.

JASON The curse of our sons' avenging spirit and of justice, that calls for blood, be on thee!

MEDEA What god or power divine hears thee, breaker of oaths and every law of hospitality?

JASON Fie upon thee! cursed witch! child-murderess!

MEDEA To thy house! go, bury thy wife.

JASON I go, bereft of both my sons.

MEDEA Thy grief is yet to come; wait till old age is with thee too.

JASON O my dear, dear children!

MEDEA Dear to their mother, not to thee.

JASON And yet thou didst slay them?

MEDEA Yea, to vex thy heart.

JASON One last fond kiss, ah me! I fain would on their lips imprint.

MEDEA Embraces now, and fond farewells for them; but then a cold repulse!

JASON By heaven I do adjure thee, let me touch their tender skin.

MEDEA No, no! in vain this word has sped its flight.

JASON O Zeus, dost hear how I am driven hence; dost mark the treatment I receive from this she-lion, fell murderess of her young? Yet so far as I may and can, I raise for them a dirge, and do adjure the gods to witness how thou hast slain my sons, and wilt not suffer me to embrace or bury their dead bodies. Would I had never begotten them to see thee slay them after all! (The chariot carries MEDEA away.)

CHORUS (chanting) Many a fate doth Zeus dispense, high on his Olympian throne; oft do the gods bring things to pass beyond man's expectation; that, which we thought would be, is not fulfilled, while for the unlooked-for god finds out a way; and such hath been the issue of this matter.

THE END

Hippolytus

Dramatis Personae

APHRODITE
HIPPOLYTUS, bastard son of THESEUS
ATTENDANTS OF HIPPOLYTUS
CHORUS OF TROEZENIAN WOMEN
NURSE OF PHAEDRA
PHAEDRA, wife of THESEUS
THESEUS
MESSENGER

Before the royal palace at Troezen. There is a statue of APHRODITE on one side; on the other, a statue of ARTEMIS. There is an altar before each image. The goddess APHRODITE appears alone.

APHRODITE Wide o'er man my realm extends, and proud the name that I, the goddess Cypris, bear, both in heaven's courts and 'mongst all those who dwell within the limits of the sea and the bounds of Atlas, beholding the sun-god's light; those that respect my power I advance to honour, but bring to ruin all who vaunt themselves at me. For even in the race of gods this feeling finds a home, even pleasure at the honour men pay them. And the truth of this I soon will show; for that son of Theseus, born of the Amazon, Hippolytus, whom holy Pittheus taught, alone of all the dwellers in this land of Troezen, calls me vilest of the deities. Love he scorns, and, as for marriage, will none of it; but Artemis, daughter of Zeus, sister of Phoebus, he doth honour, counting her the chief of goddesses, and ever through the greenwood, attendant on his virgin goddess, he clears the earth of wild beasts with his fleet hounds, enjoying the comradeship of one too high for mortal ken. 'Tis not this I grudge him, no! why should I? But for his sins against me, I will this very day take vengeance on Hippolytus; for long ago I cleared the ground of many obstacles, so it needs but trifling toil. For as he came one day from the home of Pittheus to witness the solemn mystic rites and be initiated therein in Pandion's land, Phaedra, his father's noble wife, caught sight of him, and by my designs she found her heart was seized with wild desire. And ere she came to this Troezenian realm, a temple did she rear to Cypris hard by the rock of Pallas where it o'erlooks this country, for love of the youth in another land; and to win his love in days to come she called after his name the temple she had founded for the goddess. Now, when Theseus left the land of Cecrops, flying the pollution of the blood of Pallas' sons, and with his wife sailed to this shore, content to suffer exile for a year, then began the wretched wife to pine away in silence, moaning 'neath love's cruel scourge, and none of her servants knows what disease afflicts her. But this passion of hers must not fail thus. No, I will discover the matter to Theseus, and all shall be laid bare. Then will the father slay his child, my bitter foe, by curses, for the lord Poseidon granted this boon to Theseus; three wishes of the god to ask, nor ever ask in vain. So Phaedra is to die, an honoured death 'tis true, but still to die; for I will not let her suffering outweigh the payment of such forfeit by my foes as shall satisfy my honour. But lo! I see the son of Theseus coming hither-Hippolytus, fresh from the labours of the chase. I will get me hence. At his back follows a long train of retainers, in joyous cries of revelry uniting and hymns of praise to Artemis, his goddess; for little he recks that Death hath oped his gates for him, and that this is his last look upon the light. (APHRODITE vanishes. HIPPOLYTUS and his retinue of hunting ATTENDANTS enter, singing. They move to worship at the altar of ARTEMIS.)

HIPPOLYTUS Come follow, friends, singing to Artemis,

daughter of Zeus, throned in the sky, whose votaries we are.

ATTENDANTS Lady goddess, awful queen, daughter of Zeus, all hail! hail! of Latona and of Zeus, peerless mid the virgin choir, who hast thy dwelling in heaven's wide mansions at thy noble father's court, in the golden house of Zeus. All hail! most beauteous Artemis, lovelier far than all the daughters of Olympus!

HIPPOLYTUS (speaking) For thee, O mistress mine, I bring this woven wreath, culled from a virgin meadow, where nor shepherd dares to herd his flock nor ever scythe hath mown, but o'er the mead unshorn the bee doth wing its way in spring; and with the dew from rivers drawn purity that garden tends. Such as know no cunning lore, yet in whose nature self-control, made perfect, hath a home, these may pluck the flowers, but not the wicked world. Accept, I pray, dear mistress, mine this chaplet from my holy hand to crown thy locks of gold; for I, and none other of mortals, have this high guerdon, to be with thee, with thee converse, hearing thy voice, though not thy face beholding. So be it mine to end my life as I began.

LEADER OF THE ATTENDANTS My prince! we needs must call upon the gods, our lords, so wilt thou listen to a friendly word from me?

HIPPOLYTUS Why, that will I! else were I proved a fool.

LEADER Dost know, then, the way of the world?

HIPPOLYTUS Not I; but wherefore such a question?

LEADER It hates reserve which careth not for all men's love.

HIPPOLYTUS And rightly too; reserve in man is ever galling.

LEADER But there's a charm in courtesy?

HIPPOLYTUS The greatest surely; aye, and profit, too,

at trifling cost.

LEADER Dost think the same law holds in heaven as well?

HIPPOLYTUS I trow it doth, since all our laws we men from heaven draw.

LEADER Why, then, dost thou neglect to greet an august goddess?

HIPPOLYTUS Whom speak'st thou of? Keep watch upon thy tongue lest it same mischief cause.

LEADER Cypris I mean, whose image is stationed o'er thy gate.

HIPPOLYTUS I greet her from afar, preserving still my chastity.

LEADER Yet is she an august goddess, far renowned on earth.

HIPPOLYTUS 'Mongst gods as well as men we have our several preferences.

LEADER I wish thee luck, and wisdom too, so far as thou dost need it.

HIPPOLYTUS No god, whose worship craves the night, hath charms for me.

LEADER My son, we should avail us of the gifts that gods confer.

HIPPOLYTUS Go in, my faithful followers, and make ready food within the house; a well-filled board hath charms after the chase is o'er. Rub down my steeds ye must, that when I have had my fill I may yoke them to the chariot and give them proper exercise. As for thy Queen of Love, a long farewell to her. (HIPPOLYTUS goes into the palace, followed by all the ATTENDANTS except the LEADER, who prays before the statue of APHRODITE.)

LEADER Meantime I with sober mind, for I must not

copy my young master, do offer up my prayer to thy image, lady Cypris, in such words as it becomes a slave to use. But thou should'st pardon all, who, in youth's impetuous heat, speak idle words of thee; make as though thou hearest not, for gods must needs be wiser than the sons of men. (The LEADER goes into the palace. The CHORUS OF TROEZENIAN WOMEN enters.)

CHORUS (singing, strophe 1)

A rock there is, where, as they say, the ocean dew distils, and from its beetling brow it pours a copious stream for pitchers to be dipped therein; 'twas here I had a friend washing robes of purple in the trickling stream, and she was spreading them out on the face of warm sunny rock; from her I had the tidings, first of all, that my mistress-

(antistrophe 1)

Was wasting on the bed of sickness, pent within her house, a thin veil o'ershadowing her head of golden hair. And this is the third day I hear that she hath closed her lovely lips and denied her chaste body all sustenance, eager to hide her suffering and reach death's cheerless bourn.

(strophe 2)

Maiden, thou must be possessed, by Pan made frantic or by Hecate, or by the Corybantes dread, and Cybele the mountain mother. Or maybe thou hast sinned against Dictynna, huntress-queen, and art wasting for thy guilt in sacrifice unoffered. For she doth range o'er lakes' expanse and past the bounds of earth upon the ocean's tossing billows.

(antistrophe 2)

Or doth some rival in thy house beguile thy lord, the captain of Erechtheus' sons, that hero nobly born, to secret amours hid from thee? Or hath some mariner sailing hither from Crete reached this port that sailors love, with evil tidings for our queen, and she with sorrow for her grievous fate is to her bed confined?

(epode)

Yea, and oft o'er woman's wayward nature settles a feeling of miserable helplessness, arising from pains of childbirth or of passionate desire. I, too, have felt at times this sharp thrill shoot through me, but I would cry to Artemis, queen of archery, who comes from heaven to aid us in our travail, and thanks to heaven's grace she ever comes at my call with welcome help. Look! where the aged nurse is bringing her forth from the house before the door, while on her brow the cloud of gloom is deepening. My soul longs to learn what is her grief, the canker that is wasting our queen's fading charms. (PHAEDRA is led out and placed upon a couch by the NURSE and attendants. The following lines between the NURSE and PHAEDRA are chanted.)

NURSE O, the ills of mortal men! the cruel diseases they endure! What can I do for thee? from what refrain? Here is the bright sunlight, here the azure sky; lo! we have brought thee on thy bed of sickness without the palace; for all thy talk was of coming hither, but soon back to thy chamber wilt thou hurry. Disappointment follows fast with thee, thou hast no joy in aught for long; the present has no power to please; on something absent next thy heart is set. Better be sick than tend the sick; the first is but a single ill, the last unites mental grief with manual toil. Man's whole life is full of anguish; no respite from his woes he finds; but if there is aught to love beyond this life, night's dark pall doth wrap it round. And so we show our mad love of this life because its light is shed on earth, and because we know no other, and have naught revealed to us of all our earth may hide; and trusting to fables we drift at random.

PHAEDRA (wildly) Lift my body, raise my head! My limbs are all unstrung, kind friends. O handmaids, lift my arms, my shapely arms. The tire on my head is too heavy for me to wear; away with it, and let my tresses o'er my shoulders fall.

Be of good heart, dear child; toss not so wildly to and fro. Lie still, be brave, so wilt thou find thy sickness easier to bear; suffering for mortals is nature's iron law.

PHAEDRA Ah! would I could draw a draught of water pure from some dew-fed spring, and lay me down to rest in the grassy meadow 'neath the poplar's shade!

NURSE My child, what wild speech is this? O say not such things in public, wild whirling words of frenzy bred!

PHAEDRA Away to the mountain take me! to the wood, to the pine-trees will go, where hounds pursue the prey, hard on the scent of dappled fawns. Ye gods! what joy to hark them on, to grasp the barbed dart, to poise Thessalian hunting-spears close to my golden hair, then let them fly.

NURSE Why, why, my child, these anxious cares? What hast thou to do with the chase? Why so eager for the flowing spring, when hard by these towers stands a hill well watered, whence thou may'st freely draw?

PHAEDRA O Artemis, who watchest o'er sea-beat Limna and the race-course thundering to the horse's hoofs, would I were upon thy plains curbing Venetian steeds!

NURSE Why betray thy frenzy in these wild whirling words? Now thou wert for hasting hence to the hills away to hunt wild beasts, and now thy yearning is to drive the steed over the waveless sands. This needs a cunning seer to say what god it is that reins thee from the course, distracting thy senses, child.

PHAEDRA (more sanely) Ah me! alas! what have I done? Whither have I strayed, my senses leaving? Mad, mad! stricken by some demon's curse! Woe is me! Cover my head again, nurse. Shame fills me for the words I have spoken. Hide me then; from my eyes the tear-drops stream, and for very shame I turn them away. 'Tis painful coming to one's senses again, and madness, evil though it be, has this advantage, that one has no knowledge of reason's overthrow.

NURSE There then I cover thee; but when will death hide my body in the grave? Many a lesson length of days is teaching me. Yea, mortal men should pledge themselves to moderate friendships only, not to such as reach the very heart's core; affection's ties should be light upon them to let them slip or draw them tight. For one poor heart to grieve for twain, as I do for my mistress, is a burden sore to bear. Men say that too engrossing pursuits in life more oft cause disappointment than pleasure, and too oft are foes to health. Wherefore do not praise excess so much as moderation, and with me wise men will agree. (PHAEDRA lies back upon the couch.)

LEADER OF THE CHORUS (speaking) O aged dame, faithful nurse of Phaedra, our queen, we see her sorry plight; but what it is that ails her we cannot discern, so fain would learn of thee and hear thy opinion.

NURSE I question her, but am no wiser, for she will not answer.

LEADER Nor tell what source these sorrows have?

NURSE The same answer thou must take, for she is dumb on every point.

LEADER How weak and wasted is her body!

NURSE What marvel? 'tis three days now since she has tasted food.

LEADER Is this infatuation, or an attempt to die?

NURSE 'Tis death she courts; such fasting aims at ending life.

LEADER A strange story if it satisfies her husband.

NURSE She hides from him her sorrow, and vows she is not ill.

LEADER Can he not guess it from her face?

NURSE He is not now in his own country.

LEADER But dost not thou insist in thy endeavour to find out her complaint, her mind?

NURSE I have tried every plan, and all in vain; yet not even now will I relax my zeal, that thou too, if thou stayest, mayst witness my devotion to my unhappy mistress. Come, come, my darling child, let us forget, the twain of us, our former words; be thou more mild, smoothing that sullen brow and changing the current of thy thought, and I, if in aught before failed in humouring thee, will let that be and find some better course. If thou art sick with ills thou canst not name, there be women here to help to set thee right; but if thy trouble can to men's ears be divulged, speak, that physicians may pronounce on it. Come, then, why so dumb? Thou shouldst not so remain, my child, but scold me if I speak amiss, or, if I give good counsel, yield assent. One word, one look this way! Ah me! Friends, we waste our toil to no purpose; we are as far away as ever; she would not relent to my arguments then, nor is she yielding now. Well, grow more stubborn than the sea, yet be assured of this, that if thou diest thou art a traitress to thy children, for they will ne'er inherit their father's halls, nay, by that knightly queen the Amazon who bore a son to lord it over thine, a bastard born but not a bastard bred, whom well thou knowest, e'en Hippolytus- (At the mention of his name PHAEDRA'S attention is suddenly caught.)

PHAEDRA Oh! oh!

NURSE Ha! doth that touch the quick?

PHAEDRA Thou hast undone me, nurse; I do adjure by the gods, mention that man no more.

NURSE There now! thou art thyself again, but e'en yet refusest to aid thy children and preserve thy life.

PHAEDRA My babes I love, but there is another storm that buffets me.

NURSE Daughter, are thy hands from bloodshed pure?

PHAEDRA My hands are pure, but on my soul there rests a stain.

NURSE The issue of some enemy's secret witchery?

PHAEDRA A friend is my destroyer, one unwilling as myself.

NURSE Hath Theseus wronged thee in any wise?

PHAEDRA Never may I prove untrue to himl

NURSE Then what strange mystery is there that drives thee on to die?

PHAEDRA O, let my sin and me alone, 'tis not 'gainst thee I sin.

NURSE Never willingly! and, if I fail, 'twill rest at thy door.

PHAEDRA How now? thou usest force in clinging to my hand.

NURSE Yea, and I will never loose my hold upon thy knees.

PHAEDRA Alas for thee! my sorrows, shouldst thou learn them, would recoil on thee.

NURSE What keener grief for me than failing to win thee?

PHAEDRA 'Twill be death to thee; though to me that brings renown.

NURSE And dost thou then conceal this boon despite my prayers?

PHAEDRA I do, for 'tis out of shame I am planning an honourable escape.

NURSE Tell it, and thine honour shall the brighter shine.

PHAEDRA Away, I do conjure thee; loose my hand.

NURSE I will not, for the boon thou shouldst have granted me is denied.

PHAEDRA I will grant it out of reverence for thy holy

suppliant touch.

NURSE Henceforth I hold my peace; 'tis thine to speak from now.

PHAEDRA Ah! hapless mother, what a love was thine!

NURSE Her love for the bull? daughter, or what meanest thou?

PHAEDRA And woe to thee! my sister, bride of Dionysus.

NURSE What ails thee, child? speaking ill of kith and kin.

PHAEDRA Myself the third to suffer! how am I undone!

NURSE Thou strik'st me dumb! Where will this history end?

PHAEDRA That "love" has been our curse from time long past.

NURSE I know no more of what I fain would learn.

PHAEDRA Ah! would thou couldst say for me what I have to tell.

NURSE I aw no prophetess to unriddle secrets.

PHAEDRA What is it they mean when they talk of people being in "love-"?

NURSE At once the sweetest and the bitterest thing, my child.

PHAEDRA I shall only find the latter half.

NURSE Ha! my child, art thou in love?

PHAEDRA The Amazon's son, whoever he may be-

NURSE Mean'st thou Hippolytus?

PHAEDRA 'Twas thou, not I, that spoke his name.

NURSE O heavens! what is this, my child? Thou hast ruined me. Outrageous! friends; I will not live and bear it; hateful is life, hateful to mine eyes the light. This body I resign, will cast it off, and rid me of existence by my death. Farewell, my life is o'er. Yea, for the chaste I have wicked passions, 'gainst their will maybe, but still they have. Cypris, it seems, is not goddess after all, but something greater far, for she hath been the ruin of my lady and of me and our whole family.

CHORUS (chanting) O, too clearly didst thou hear our queen uplift her voice to tell her startling tale of piteous suffering. Come death ere I reach thy state of feeling, loved mistress. O horrible! woe, for these miseries! woe, for the sorrows on which mortals feed! Thou art undone! thou hast disclosed thy sin to heaven's light. What hath each passing day and every hour in store for thee? Some strange event will come to pass in this house. For it is no longer uncertain where the star of thy love is setting, thou hapless daughter of Crete.

PHAEDRA Women of Troezen, who dwell here upon the frontier edge of Pelops' land, oft ere now in heedless mood through the long hours of night have I wondered why man's life is spoiled; and it seems to me their evil case is not due to any natural fault of judgment, for there be many dowered with sense, but we must view the matter in this light: by teaching and experience to learn the right but neglect it in practice, some from sloth, others from preferring pleasure of some kind or other to duty. Now life has many pleasures, protracted talk, and leisure, that seductive evil; likewise there is shame which is of two kinds, one a noble quality, the other a curse to families; but if for each its proper time were clearly known, these twain could not have had the selfsame letters to denote them. So then since I had made up my mind on these points, 'twas not likely any drug would alter it and make me think the contrary. And I will tell the too the way my judgment went. When love wounded me, I bethought me how I best might bear the smart. So from that day forth I began to hide in silence what I suffered. For I put no faith in counsellors, who know well to lecture others for presumption, yet themselves have countless troubles of their own. Next I did devise noble endurance of these wanton thoughts, striving by continence for victory. And last when I could not succeed in mastering love hereby, methought it best to die; and none can gainsay my purpose. For fain I would my virtue should to all appear, my shame have few to witness it. I knew my sickly passion now; to yield to it I saw how infamous; and more, I learnt to know so well that I was but woman, a thing the world detests. Curses, hideous curses on that wife who first did shame her marriage-vow for lovers other than her lord! 'Twas from noble families this curse began to spread among our sex. For when the noble countenance disgrace, poor folk of course will think that it is right. Those too I hate who make profession of purity, though in secret reckless sinners. How can these, queen Cypris, ocean's child, e'er look their husbands in the face? do they never feel one guilty thrill that their accomplice, night, or the chambers of their house will find a voice and speak? This it is that calls on me to die, kind friends, that so I may ne'er be found to have disgraced my lord, or the children I have borne; no! may they grow up and dwell in glorious Athens, free to speak and act, heirs to such fair fame as a mother can bequeath. For to know that father or mother has sinned doth turn the stoutest heart to slavishness. This alone, men say, can stand the buffets of life's battle, a just and virtuous soul in whomsoever found. For time unmasks the villain soon or late, holding up to them a mirror as to some blooming maid. 'Mongst such may I be never seen!

LEADER OF THE CHORUS Now look! how fair is chastity however viewed, whose fruit is good repute amongst men.

NURSE My queen, 'tis true thy tale of woe, but lately told, did for the moment strike me with wild alarm, but now I do reflect upon my foolishness; second thoughts are often best even with men. Thy fate is no uncommon nor past one's calculations; thou art stricken by the passion Cypris sends. Thou art in love; what wonder? so are many more. Wilt thou, because thou lov'st, destroy thyself? 'Tis little gain, I trow, for those who love or yet may love their fellows, if death must be their end; for though the Love-Queen's onset in her might is more than man can bear, yet doth she gently visit yielding hearts, and only when she finds a proud unnatural spirit, doth she take and mock it past belief. Her path is in the sky, and mid the ocean's surge she rides; from her all nature springs; she sows the seeds of love, inspires the warm desire to which we sons of earth all owe our being. They who have aught to do with books of ancient scribes, or themselves engage in studious pursuits, know how Zeus of Semele was enamoured, how the bright-eyed goddess of the Dawn once stole Cephalus to dwell in heaven for the love she bore him; yet these in heaven abide nor shun the gods' approach, content, I trow, to yield to their misfortune. Wilt thou refuse to yield? thy sire, it seems, should have begotten thee on special terms or with different gods for masters, if in these laws thou wilt not acquiesce. How many, prithee, men of sterling sense, when they see their wives unfaithful, make as though they saw it not? How many fathers, when their sons have gone astray, assist them in their amours? 'Tis part of human wisdom to conceal the deed of shame. Nor should man aim at too great refinement in his life; for they cannot with exactness finish e'en the roof that covers in a house; and how dost thou, after falling into so deep a pit, think to escape? Nay, if thou hast more of good than bad, thou wilt fare exceeding well, thy human nature considered. O cease, my darling child, from evil thoughts, let wanton pride be gone, for this is naught else, this wish to rival gods in perfectness. Face thy love; 'tis heaven's will thou shouldst. Sick thou art, yet turn thy sickness to some happy issue. For there are charms and spells to soothe the soul; surely some cure for thy disease will be found. Men, no doubt, might seek it long and late if our women's minds no scheme devise.

LEADER Although she gives thee at thy present need the wiser counsel, Phaedra, yet do I praise thee. Still my praise may sound more harsh and jar more cruelly on thy ear than her advice.

PHAEDRA 'Tis even this, too plausible a tongue, that

overthrows good governments and homes of men. We should not speak to please the ear but point the path that leads to noble fame.

NURSE What means this solemn speech? Thou needst not rounded phrases,-but a man. Straightway must we move to tell him frankly how it is with thee. Had not thy life to such a crisis come, or wert thou with self-control I endowed, ne'er would I to gratify thy passions have urged thee to this course; but now 'tis a struggle fierce to save thy life, and therefore less to blame.

PHAEDRA Accursed proposal! peace, woman! never utter those shameful words again!

NURSE Shameful, maybe, yet for thee better than honour's code. Better this deed, if it shall save thy life, than that name thy pride will kill thee to retain.

PHAEDRA I conjure thee, go no further! for thy words are plausible but infamous; for though as yet love has not undermined my soul, yet, if in specious words thou dress thy foul suggestion, I shall be beguiled into the snare from which I am now escaping.

NURSE If thou art of this mind, 'twere well thou ne'er hadst sinned; but as it is, hear me; for that is the next best course; I in my house have charms to soothe thy love,-'twas but now I thought of them;-these shall cure thee of thy sickness on no disgraceful terms, thy mind unhurt, if thou wilt be but brave. But from him thou lovest we must get some token, word or fragment of his robe, and thereby unite in one love's twofold stream.

PHAEDRA Is thy drug a salve or potion?

NURSE I cannot tell; be content, my child, to profit by it and ask no questions.

PHAEDRA I fear me thou wilt prove too wise for me.

NURSE If thou fear this, confess thyself afraid of all; but why thy terror!

PHAEDRA Lest thou shouldst breathe a word of this to Theseus' son.

NURSE Peace, my child! I will do all things well; only be thou, queen Cypris, ocean's child, my partner in the work! And for the rest of my purpose, it will be enough for me to tell it to our friends within the house. (The NURSE goes into the palace.)

CHORUS (singing, strophe 1)

O Love, Love, that from the eyes diffusest soft desire, bringing on the souls of those, whom thou dost camp against, sweet grace, O never in evil mood appear to me, nor out of time and tune approach! Nor fire nor meteor hurls a mightier bolt than Aphrodite's shaft shot by the hands of Love, the child of Zeus.

(antistrophe 1)

Idly, idly by the streams of Alpheus and in the Pythian shrines of Phoebus, Hellas heaps the slaughtered steers; while Love we worship not, Love, the king of men, who holds the key to Aphrodite's sweetest bower,-worship not him who, when he comes, lays waste and marks his path to mortal hearts by wide-spread woe.

(strophe 2)

There was that maiden in Oechalia, a girl unwed, that knew no wooer yet nor married joys; her did the Queen of Love snatch from her home across the sea and gave unto Alcmena's son, mid blood and smoke and murderous marriage-hymns, to be to him a frantic fiend of hell; woe! woe for his wooing!

(antistrophe 2)

Ah! holy walls of Thebes, ah! fount of Dirce, ye could testify what course the love-queen follows. For with the blazing levin-bolt did she cut short the fatal marriage of Semele, mother of Zeus-born Bacchus. All things she doth inspire, dread goddess, winging her flight hither and thither like a bee.

PHAEDRA Peace, oh women, peace! I am undone.

LEADER OF THE CHORUS What, Phaedra, is this dread event within thy house?

PHAEDRA Hush! let me hear what those within are saying.

LEADER I am silent; this is surely the prelude to evil.

PHAEDRA (chanting) Great gods! how awful are my sufferings!

CHORUS (chanting) What a cry was there! what loud alarm! say what sudden terror, lady, doth thy soul dismay.

PHAEDRA I am undone. Stand here at the door and hear the noise arising in the house.

CHORUS (chanting) Thou art already by the bolted door; 'tis for thee to note the sounds that issue from within. And tell me, O tell me what evil can be on foot.

PHAEDRA 'Tis the son of the horse-loving Amazon who calls, Hippolytus, uttering foul curses on my servant.

CHORUS (chanting) I hear a noise but cannot dearly tell which way it comes. Ah! 'tis through the door the sound reached thee.

PHAEDRA Yes, yes, he is calling her plainly enough a go-between in vice, traitress to her master's honour.

CHORUS (chanting) Woe, woe is me! thou art betrayed, dear mistress! What counsel shall I give thee? thy secret is out; thou art utterly undone.

PHAEDRA Ah me! ah me!

CHORUS (chanting) Betrayed by friends!

PHAEDRA She hath ruined me by speaking of my misfortune; 'twas kindly meant, but an ill way to cure my malady.

LEADER OF THE CHORUS O what wilt thou do now in thy cruel dilemma?

PHAEDRA I only know one way, one cure for these my woes, and that is instant death. (HIPPOLYTUS bursts out of the palace, followed closely by the NURSE.)

HIPPOLYTUS O mother earth! O sun's unclouded orb! What words, unfit for any lips, have reached my ears!

NURSE Peace, my son, lest some one hear thy outcry.

HIPPOLYTUS I cannot hear such awful words and hold my peace.

NURSE I do implore thee by thy fair right hand.

HIPPOLYTUS Let go my hand, touch not my robe.

NURSE O by thy knees I pray, destroy me not utterly.

HIPPOLYTUS Why say this, if, as thou pretendest, thy lips are free from blame?

NURSE My son, this is no story to be noised abroad.

HIPPOLYTUS A virtuous tale grows fairer told to many.

NURSE Never dishonour thy oath, my son.

HIPPOLYTUS My tongue an oath did take, but not my heart.

NURSE My son, what wilt thou do? destroy thy friends?

HIPPOLYTUS Friends indeed! the wicked are no friends of mine.

NURSE O pardon me; to err is only human, child.

HIPPOLYTUS Great Zeus, why didst thou, to man's sorrow, put woman, evil counterfeit, to dwell where shines the sun? If thou wert minded that the human race should multiply, it was not from women they should have drawn their stock, but in thy temples they should have paid gold or iron or ponderous bronze and bought a family, each man proportioned to his offering, and so in independence dwelt, from women free. But now as soon as ever we would bring this plague into our home we bring its fortune to the ground. 'Tis clear from this how great a curse a woman is; the very father, that begot and nurtured her, to rid him of the mischief, gives her a dower and packs her off; while the husband, who takes the noxious weed into his home, fondly decks his sorry idol in fine raiment and tricks her out in robes, squandering by degrees, unhappy wight! his house's wealth. For he is in this dilemma; say his marriage has brought him good connections, he is glad then to keep the wife he loathes; or, if he gets a good wife but useless kin, he tries to stifle the bad luck with the good. But it is easiest for him who has settled in his house as wife mere cipher, incapable from simplicity. I hate a clever woman; never may she set foot in my house who aims at knowing more than women need; for in these clever women Cypris implants a larger store of villainy, while the artless woman is by her shallow wit from levity debarred. No servant should ever have had access to a wife, but men should put to live with them beasts, which bite, not talk, in which case they could not speak to any one nor be answered back by them. But, as it is, the wicked in their chambers plot wickedness, and their servants carry it abroad. Even thus, vile wretch, thou cam'st to make me partner in an outrage on my father's honour; wherefore I must wash that stain away in running streams, dashing the water into my ears. How could I commit so foul a crime when by the very mention of it I feel myself polluted? Be well assured, woman, 'tis only my religious scruple saves thee. For had not I unawares been caught by an oath, 'fore heaven! I would not have refrained from telling all unto my father. But now I will from the house away, so long as Theseus is abroad, and will maintain strict silence. But, when my father comes, I will return and see how thou and thy mistress face him, and so shall I learn by experience the extent of thy audacity. Perdition seize you both! I can never satisfy my hate for women, no! not even though some say this is ever my theme, for of a truth they always are evil. So either let some one prove them chaste, or let me still trample on them for ever. (HIPPOLYTUS departs in anger.)

CHORUS (chanting) O the cruel, unhappy fate of women! What arts, what arguments have we, once we have made a slip, to loose by craft the tight-drawn knot?

PHAEDRA (chanting) I have met my deserts. O earth, O light of day! How can I escape the stroke of fate? How my pangs conceal, kind friends? What god will appear to help me, what mortal to take my part or help me in unrighteousness? The present calamity of my life admits of no escape. Most hapless I of all my sex!

LEADER OF THE CHORUS Alas, alas! the deed is done, thy servant's schemes have gone awry, my queen, and all is lost.

PHAEDRA (to the NURSE) Accursed woman! traitress to thy friends! How hast thou ruined me! May Zeus, my ancestor, smite thee with his fiery bolt and uproot thee from thy place. Did I not foresee thy purpose, did I not bid thee keep silence on the very matter which is now my shame? But thou wouldst not be still; wherefore my fair name will not go with me to the tomb. But now I must another scheme devise. Yon youth, in the keenness of his fury, will tell his father of my sin, and the aged Pittheus of my state and fill the world with stories to my shame. Perdition seize thee and every meddling fool who by dishonest means would serve unwilling friends!

NURSE Mistress, thou may'st condemn the mischief I have done, for sorrow's sting o'ermasters thy judgment; yet can I answer thee in face of this, if thou wilt hear. 'Twas I who nurtured thee; I love thee still; but in my search for medicine to cure thy sickness I found what least I sought. Had I but succeeded, I had been counted wise, for the credit we get for wisdom is measured by our success.

PHAEDRA Is it just, is it any satisfaction to me, that thou shouldst wound me first, then bandy words with me?

NURSE We dwell on this too long; I was not wise, I own;

but there are yet ways of escape from the trouble, my child.

PHAEDRA Be dumb henceforth; evil was thy first advice to me, evil too thy attempted scheme. Begone and leave me, look to thyself; I will my own fortunes for the best arrange. (The NURSE goes into the palace.) Ye noble daughters of Troezen, grant me the only boon I crave; in silence bury what ye here have heard.

LEADER By majestic Artemis, child of Zeus, I swear I will never divulge aught of thy sorrows.

PHAEDRA 'Tis well. But I, with all my thought, can but one way discover out of this calamity, that so I may secure my children's honour, and find myself some help as matters stand. For never, never will I bring shame upon my Cretan home, nor will I, to save one poor life, face Theseus after my disgrace.

LEADER Art thou bent then on some cureless woe?

PHAEDRA On death; the means thereto must I devise myself.

LEADER Hush!

PHAEDRA Do thou at least advise me well. For this very day shall I gladden Cypris, my destroyer, by yielding up my life, and shall own myself vanquished by cruel love. Yet shall my dying be another's curse, that he may learn not to exult at my misfortunes; but when he comes to share the self-same plague with me, he will take a lesson in wisdom. (PHAEDRA enters the palace.)

CHORUS (chanting, strophe 1)

O to be nestling 'neath some pathless cavern, there by god's creating hand to grow into a bird amid the winged tribes! Away would I soar to Adria's wave-beat shore and to the waters of Eridanus; where a father's hapless daughters in their grief for Phaethon distil into the glooming flood the amber brilliance of their tears.

(antistrophe 1)

And to the apple-bearing strand of those minstrels in the west then would come, where ocean's lord no more to sailors grants passage o'er the deep dark main, finding there the heaven's holy bound, upheld by Atlas, where water from ambrosial founts wells up beside the couch of Zeus inside his halls, and holy earth, the bounteous mother, causes joy to spring in heavenly breasts.

(strophe 2)

O white-winged bark, that o'er the booming ocean-wave didst bring my royal mistress from her happy home, to crown her queen 'mongst sorrow's brides! Surely evil omens from either port, at least from Crete, were with that ship, what time to glorious Athens it sped its way, and the crew made fast its twisted cable-ends upon the beach of Munychus, and on the land stept out.

(antistrophe 2)

Whence comes it that her heart is crushed, cruelly afflicted by Aphrodite with unholy love; so she by bitter grief o'erwhelmed will tie a noose within her bridal bower to fit it to her fair white neck, to modest for this hateful lot in life, prizing o'er all her name and fame, and striving thus to rid her soul of passion's sting. (The NURSE rushes out of the palace.)

NURSE Help! ho! To the rescue all who near the palace stand! She hath hung herself, our queen, the wife of Theseus.

LEADER OF THE CHORUS Woe worth the day! the deed is done; our royal mistress is no more, dead she hangs in the dangling noose.

NURSE Haste! some one bring a two-edged knife wherewith to cut the knot about her neck.

FIRST SEMI-CHORUS Friends, what shall we do? think you we should enter the house, and loose the queen from the tight-drawn noose?

SECOND SEMI-CHORUS Why should we? Are there not young servants here? To do too much is not a safe course in life.

NURSE Lay out the hapless corpse, straighten the limbs. This was a bitter way to sit at home and keep my master's house! (She goes in.)

LEADER OF THE CHORUS She is dead, poor lady; 'tis this I hear. Already are they laying out the corpse. (THESEUS and his retinue have entered, unnoticed.)

THESEUS Women, can ye tell me what the uproar in the palace means? There came the sound of servants weeping bitterly to mine ear. None of my household deign to open wide the gates and give me glad welcome as traveller from prophetic shrines. Hath aught befallen old Pittheus? No, Though he be well advanced in years, yet should I mourn, were he to quit this house.

LEADER 'Tis not against the old, Theseus, that fate, to strike thee, aims this blow; prepare thy sorrow for a younger corpse.

THESEUS Woe is me! is it a child's life death robs me of?

LEADER They live; but, cruellest news of all for thee, their mother is no more.

THESEUS What! my wife dead? By what cruel stroke of chance?

LEADER About her neck she tied the hangman's knot.

THESEUS Had grief so chilled her blood? or what had befallen her?

LEADER I know but this, for I am myself but now arrived at the house to mourn thy sorrows, O Theseus.

THESEUS Woe is me! why have I crowned my head with

woven garlands, when misfortune greets my embassage? Unbolt the doors, servants, loose their fastenings, that I may see the piteous sight, my wife, whose death is death to me. (The central doors of the palace open, disclosing the corpse.) Woe! woe is thee for thy piteous lot! thou hast done thyself a hurt deep enough to overthrow this family. Ah! ah! the daring of it done to death by violence and unnatural means, the desperate effort of thy own poor hand! Who cast the shadow o'er thy life, poor lady?

THESEUS (chanting) Ah me, my cruel lot! sorrow hath done her worst on me. O fortune, how heavily hast thou set thy foot on me and on my house, by fiendish hands inflicting an unexpected stain? Nay, 'tis complete effacement of my life, making it not to be lived; for I see, alas! so wide an ocean of grief that I can never swim to shore again, nor breast the tide of this calamity. How shall I speak of thee, my poor wife, what tale of direst suffering tell? Thou art vanished like a bird from the covert of my hand, taking one headlong leap from me to Hades' halls. Alas, and woe! this is a bitter, bitter sight! This must be a judgment sent by God for the sins of an ancestor, which from some far source I am bringing on myself.

LEADER OF THE CHORUS My prince, 'tis not to thee alone such sorrows come; thou hast lost a noble wife, but so have many others.

THESEUS (chanting) Fain would I go hide me 'neath earth's blackest depth, to dwell in darkness with the dead in misery, now that I am reft of thy dear presence! for thou hast slain me than thyself e'en more. Who can tell me what caused the fatal stroke that reached thy heart, dear wife? Will no one tell me what befell? doth my palace all in vain give shelter to a herd of menials? Woe, woe for thee, my wife! sorrows past speech, past bearing, I behold within my house; myself ruined man, my home a solitude, my children orphans!

CHORUS (chanting) Gone and left us hast thou, fondest wife and noblest of all women 'neath the sun's bright eye or night's star-lit radiance. Poor house, what sorrows are thy portion now! My eyes are wet with streams of tears to see thy fate; but the ill that is to follow has long with terror filled me.

THESEUS Ha! what means this letter? clasped in her dear hand it hath some strange tale to tell. Hath she, poor lady, as a last request, written her bidding as to my marriage and her children? Take heart, poor ghost; no wife henceforth shall wed thy Theseus or invade his house. Ah! how yon en ring affects my sight! Come, I will unfold the sealed packet and read her letter's message to me.

CHORUS (chanting) Woe unto us! Here is yet another evil in the train by heaven sent. Looking to what has happened, I should count my lot in life no longer worth one's while to gain. My master's house, alas! is ruined, brought to naught, I say. Spare it, O Heaven, if it may be. Hearken to my prayer, for I see, as with prophetic eye, an omen boding ill.

THESEUS O horror! woe on woe! and still they come, too deep for words, to heavy to bear. Ah me!

LEADER OF THE CHORUS What is it? speak, if I may share in it.

THESEUS (chanting) This letter loudly tells a hideous tale! where can I escape my load of woe? For I am ruined and undone, so awful are the words I find here written clear as if she cried them to me; woe is me!

LEADER Alas! thy words declare themselves the harbingers of woe.

THESEUS I can no longer keep the cursed tale within the portal of my lips, cruel though its utterance be. Ah me! Hippolytus hath dared by brutal force to violate my honour, recking naught of Zeus, whose awful eye is over all. O father Poseidon, once didst thou promise to fulfil three prayers of mine; answer one of these and slay my son, let him not escape this single day, if the prayers thou gavest me were indeed with issue fraught.

LEADER O king, I do conjure thee, call back that prayer; hereafter thou wilt know thy error. Hear, I pray.

THESEUS It cannot be! Moreover I will banish him from this land, and by one of two fates shall he be struck down; either Poseidon, out of respect to my prayer, will cast his dead body into the house of Hades; or exiled from this land, a wanderer to some foreign shore, shall he eke out a life of misery.

LEADER Lo! where himself doth come, thy son Hippolytus, in good time; dismiss thy hurtful rage, King Theseus, and bethink thee what is best for thy house, (HIPPOLYTUS enters.)

HIPPOLYTUS I heard thy voice, father, and hasted to come hither; yet know I not the cause of thy present sorrow, but would fain learn of thee. (He sees PHAEDRA'S body.) Ha! what is this? thy wife is dead? 'Tis very strange; it was but now I left her; a moment since she looked upon the light. How came she thus? the manner of her death? this would I learn of thee, father. Art dumb? silence availeth not in trouble; nay, for the heart that fain would know all must show its curiosity even in sorrow's hour. Be sure it is not right, father, to hide misfortunes from those who love, ay, more than love thee.

THESEUS O ye sons of men, victims of a thousand idle errors, why teach your countless crafts, why scheme and seek to find a way for everything, while one thing ye know not nor ever yet have made your prize, a way to teach them wisdom whose souls are void of sense?

HIPPOLYTUS A very master in his craft the man, who can force fools to be wise! But these ill-timed subtleties of thine, father, make me fear thy tongue is running wild through trouble.

THESEUS Fie upon thee! man needs should have some certain test set up to try his friends, some touchstone of their hearts, to know each friend whether he be true or false; all men should have two voices, one the voice of honesty, expediency's the other, so would honesty confute its knavish opposite, and then we could not be deceived.

HIPPOLYTUS Say, hath some friend been slandering me and hath he still thine ear? and I, though guiltless, banned? I am amazed, for thy random, frantic words fill me with wild alarm.

THESEUS O the mind of mortal man! to what lengths will it proceed? What limit will its bold assurance have? for if it goes on growing as man's life advances, and each successor outdo the man before him in villainy, the gods will have to add another sphere unto the world, which shall take in the knaves and villians. Behold this man; he, my own son, hath outraged mine honour, his guilt most clearly proved by my dead wife. Now, since thou hast dared this loathly crime, come, look thy father in the face. Art thou the man who dost with gods consort, as one above the vulgar herd? art thou the chaste and sinless saint? Thy boasts will never persuade me to be guilty of attributing ignorance to gods. Go then, vaunt thyself, and drive thy petty trade in viands formed of lifeless food; take Orpheus for thy chief and go a-revelling, with all honour for the vapourings of many a written scroll, seeing thou now art caught. Let all beware, I say, of such hypocrites! who hunt their prey with fine words, and all the while are scheming villainy. She is dead; dost think that this will save thee? Why this convicts thee more than all, abandoned wretch! What oaths, what pleas can outweigh this letter, so that thou shouldst 'scape thy doom? Thou wilt assert she hated thee, that 'twixt the bastard and the true-born child nature has herself put war; it seems then by thy showing she made a sorry bargain with her life, if to gratify her hate of thee she lost what most she prized. 'Tis said, no doubt, that frailty finds no place in man but is innate in woman; my experience is, young men are no more secure than women, whenso the Queen of Love excites a youthful breast; although their sex comes in to help them. Yet why do I thus bandy words with thee, when before me lies the corpse, to be the clearest witness? Begone at once, an exile from this land, and ne'er set foot again in god-built Athens nor in the confines of my dominion. For if I am tamely to submit to this treatment from such as thee, no more will Sinis, robber of the Isthmus, bear me witness how I slew him, but say my boasts are idle, nor will those rocks Scironian, that fringe the sea, call me the miscreants' scourge.

LEADER I know not how to call happy any child of man; for that which was first has turned and now is last.

HIPPOLYTUS Father, thy wrath and the tension of thy mind are terrible; yet this charge, specious though its arguments appear, becomes a calumny, if one lay it bare. Small skill have I in speaking to a crowd, but have a readier wit for comrades of mine own age and small companies. Yea, and this is as it should be; for they, whom the wise despise, are better qualified to speak before a mob. Yet am I constrained under the present circumstances to break silence. And at the outset will I take the point which formed the basis of thy stealthy attack on me, designed to put me out of court unheard; dost see yon sun, this earth? These do not contain, for all thou dost deny it, chastity surpassing mine. To reverence God I count the highest knowledge, and to adopt as friends not those who attempt injustice, but such as would blush to propose to their companions aught disgraceful or pleasure them by shameful services; to mock at friends is not my way, father, but I am still the same behind their backs as to their face. The very crime thou thinkest to catch me in, is just the one I am untainted with, for to this day have I kept me pure from women. Nor know I aught thereof, save what I hear or see in pictures, for I have no wish to look even on these, so pure my virgin soul. I grant my claim to chastity may not convince thee; well, 'tis then for thee to show the way I was corrupted. Did this woman exceed in beauty all her sex? Did aspire to fill the husband's place after thee and succeed to thy house? That surely would have made me out a fool, a creature void of sense. Thou wilt say, "Your chaste man loves to lord it." No, no! say I, sovereignty pleases only those whose hearts are quite corrupt. Now, I would be the first and best at all the games in Hellas, but second in the state, for ever happy thus with the noblest for my friends. For there one may be happy, and the absence of danger gives a charm beyond all princely joys. One thing I have not said, the rest thou hast. Had I a witness to attest my purity, and were I pitted 'gainst her still alive, facts would show thee on enquiry who the culprit was. Now by Zeus, the god of oaths, and by the earth, whereon we stand, I swear to thee I never did lay hand upon thy wife nor would have wished to, or have harboured such a thought. Slay me, ye gods! rob me of name and honour, from home and city cast me forth, a wandering exile o'er the earth! nor sea nor land receive my bones when I am dead, if I am such a miscreant! I cannot say if she through fear destroyed herself, for more than this am I forbid. With her discretion took the place of chastity, while I, though chaste, was not discreet in using this virtue.

LEADER Thy oath by heaven, strong security, sufficiently refutes the charge.

THESEUS A wizard or magician must the fellow be, to think he can first flout me, his father, then by coolness master my resolve.

HIPPOLYTUS Father, thy part in this doth fill me with amaze; wert thou my son and I thy sire, by heaven! I would have slain, not let thee off with banishment, hadst thou presumed to violate my honour.

THESEUS A just remark! yet shalt thou not die by the sentence thine own lips pronounce upon thyself; for death, that cometh in a moment, is an easy end for wretchedness. Nay, thou shalt be exiled from thy fatherland, and wandering to a foreign shore drag out a life of misery, for such are the wages of sin.

HIPPOLYTUS Oh! what wilt thou do? Wilt thou banish me, without so much as waiting for Time's evidence on my case?

THESEUS Ay, beyond the sea, beyond the bounds of Atlas, if I could, so deeply do I hate thee.

HIPPOLYTUS What! banish me untried, without even

testing my oath, the pledge offer, or the voice of seers?

THESEUS This letter here, though it bears no seers' signs, arraigns thy pledges; as for birds that fly o'er our heads, a long farewell to them.

HIPPOLYTUS (aside) Great gods! why do I not unlock my lips, seeing that I am ruined by you, the objects of my reverence? No, I will not; I should nowise persuade those whom I ought to, and in vain should break the oath I swore.

THESEUS Fie upon thee! that solemn air of thine is more than I can bear. Begone from thy native land forthwith!

HIPPOLYTUS Whither shall I turn? Ah me! whose friendly house will take me in, an exile on so grave, a charge?

THESEUS Seek one who loves to entertain as guests and partners in his crimes corrupters of men's wives.

HIPPOLYTUS Ah me! this wounds my heart and brings me nigh to tears to think that I should appear so vile, and thou believe me so.

THESEUS Thy tears and forethought had been more in season when thou didst presume to outrage thy father's wife.

HIPPOLYTUS O house, I would thou couldst speak for me and witness if I am so vile!

THESEUS Dost fly to speechless witnesses? This deed, though it speaketh not, proves thy guilt clearly.

HIPPOLYTUS Alas! Would I could stand and face myself, so should I weep to see the sorrows I endure.

THESEUS Ay, 'tis thy character to honour thyself far more than reverence thy parents, as thou shouldst.

HIPPOLYTUS Unhappy mother! son of sorrow! Heaven keep all friends of mine from bastard birth!

THESEUS Ho! servants, drag him hence! You heard my proclamation long ago condemning him to exile.

HIPPOLYTUS Whoso of them doth lay a hand on me shall rue it; thyself expel me, if thy spirit move thee, from the land.

THESEUS I will, unless my word thou straight obey; no pity for thy exile steals into my heart. (THESEUS goes in. The central doors of the palace are closed.)

HIPPOLYTUS The sentence then, it seems, is passed. Ah, misery! How well I know the truth herein, but know no way to tell it! O daughter of Latona, dearest to me of all deities, partner, comrade in the chase, far from glorious Athens must I fly. Farewell, city and land of Erechtheus; farewell, Troezen, most joyous home wherein to pass the spring of life; 'tis my last sight of thee, farewell! Come, my comrades in this land, young like me, greet me kindly and escort me forth, for never will ye behold a purer soul, for all my father's doubts. (HIPPOLYTUS departs. Many follow him.)

CHORUS (singing, strophe 1)

In very deed the thoughts I have about the gods, whenso they come into my mind, do much to soothe its grief, but though I cherish secret hopes of some great guiding will, yet am I at fault when survey the fate and doings of the sons of men; change succeeds to change, and man's life veers and shifts in endless restlessness.

(antistrophe 1)

Fortune grant me this, I pray, at heaven's hand,-a happy lot in life and a soul from sorrow free; opinions let me hold not too precise nor yet too hollow; but, lightly changing my habits to each morrow as it comes, may I thus attain a life of bliss!

(strophe 2)

For now no more is my mind free from doubts, unlooked-for sights greet my vision; for lo! I see the morning star of Athens, eye of Hellas, driven by his father's fury to another land. Mourn, ye sands of my native shores, ye oak-groves on the hills, where with his fleet hounds he would hunt the quarry to the death, attending on Dictynna, awful queen.

(antistrophe 2)

No more will he mount his car drawn by Venetian steeds, filling the course round Limna with the prancing of his trained horses. Nevermore in his father's house shall he wake the Muse that never slept beneath his lute-strings; no hand will crown the spots where rests the maiden Latona 'mid the boskage deep; nor evermore shall our virgins vie to win thy love, now thou art banished.

(epode)

While I with tears at thy unhappy fate shall endure a lot all undeserved. Ah! hapless mother, in vain didst thou bring forth, it seems. I am angered with the gods; out upon them! O ye linked Graces, why are ye sending from his native land this poor youth, guiltless sufferer, far from his home?

LEADER OF THE CHORUS But lo! I see a servant of Hippolytus hasting with troubled looks towards the palace. (A MESSENGER enters.)

MESSENGER Ladies, where may I find Theseus, king of the country? pray, tell me if ye know; is he within the palace here?

LEADER Lo! himself approaches from the palace. (THESEUS enters.)

MESSENGER Theseus, I am the bearer of troublous tidings to thee and all citizens who dwell in Athens or the bounds of Troezen.

THESEUS How now? hath some strange calamity o'ertaken these two neighbouring cities?

MESSENGER In one brief word, Hippolytus is dead. 'Tis true one slender thread still links him to the light of life.

THESEUS Who slew him? Did some husband come to blows with him, one whose wife, like mine, had suffered brutal violence?

MESSENGER He perished through those steeds that drew his chariot and through the curses thou didst utter, praying to thy sire, the ocean-king, to slay thy son.

THESEUS Ye gods and king Poseidon, thou hast proved my parentage by hearkening to my prayer! Say how he perished; how fell the uplifted hand of justice to smite the villain who dishonoured me?

MESSENGER Hard by the wave-beat shore were we combing out his horses' manes, weeping the while, for one had come to say that Hippolytus was harshly exiled by thee and nevermore would return to set foot in this land. Then came he, telling the same doleful tale to us upon the beach, and with him was a countless throng of friends who followed after. At length he stayed his lamentation and spake: "Why weakly rave on this wise? My father's commands must be obeyed. Ho! servants, harness my horses to the chariot; this is no longer now city of mine." Thereupon each one of us bestirred himself, and, ere a man could say 'twas done, we had the horses standing ready at our master's side. Then he caught up the reins from the chariot-rail, first fitting his feet exactly in the hollows made for them. But first with outspread palms he called upon the gods, "O Zeus, now strike me dead, if I have sinned, and let my father learn how he is wronging me, in death at least, if not in life." Therewith he seized the whip and lashed each horse in turn; while we, close by his chariot, near the reins, kept up with him along the road that leads direct to Argos and Epidaurus. And just as we were coming to a desert spot, a strip of sand beyond the borders of this country, sloping right to the Saronic gulf, there issued thence a deep rumbling sound, as it were an earthquake, fearsome noise, and the horses reared their heads and pricked their ears, while we were filled with wild alarm to know whence came the sound; when, as we gazed toward the wave-beat shore, a wave tremendous we beheld towering to the skies, so that from our view the cliffs of Sciron vanished, for it hid the isthmus and the rock of Asclepius; then swelling and frothing with a crest of foam, the sea discharged it toward the beach where stood the harnessed car, and in the moment that it broke, that mighty wall of waters, there issued from the wave a monstrous bull, whose bellowing filled the land with fearsome echoes, a sight too awful as it seemed to us who witnessed it. A panic seized the horses there and then, but our master, to horses' ways quite used, gripped in both hands his reins, and tying them to his body pulled them backward as the sailor pulls his oar; but the horses gnashed the forged bits between their teeth and bore him wildly on, regardless of their master's guiding hand or rein or jointed car. And oft as he would take the guiding rein and steer for softer ground, showed that bull in front to turn him back again, maddening his team with terror; but if in their frantic career they ran towards the rocks, he would draw nigh the chariot-rail, keeping up with them, until, suddenly dashing the wheel against a stone, he upset and wrecked the car; then was dire confusion, axle-boxes and linchpins springing into the air. While he, poor youth, entangled in the reins was dragged along, bound by a stubborn knot, his poor head dashed against the rocks, his flesh all torn, the while he cried out piteously, "Stay, stay, my horses whom my own hand hath fed at the manger, destroy me not utterly. O luckless curse of a father! Will no one come and save me for all my virtue?" Now we, though much we longed to help, were left far behind. At last, I know not how, he broke loose from the shapely reins that bound him, a faint breath of life still in him; but the horses disappeared, and that portentous bull, among the rocky ground, I know not where. I am but a slave in thy house, 'tis true, O king, yet will I never believe so monstrous a charge against thy son's character, no! not though the whole race of womankind should hang itself, or one should fill with writing every pine-tree tablet grown on Ida, sure as I am of his uprightness.

LEADER Alas! new troubles come to plague us, nor is there any escape from fate and necessity.

THESEUS My hatred for him who hath thus suffered made me glad at thy tidings, yet from regard for the gods and him, because he is my son, I feel neither joy nor sorrow at his sufferings.

MESSENGER But say, are we to bring the victim hither, or how are we to fulfil thy wishes? Bethink thee; if by me thou wilt be schooled, thou wilt not harshly treat thy son in his sad plight.

THESEUS Bring him hither, that when I see him face to face, who hath denied having polluted my wife's honour, I may by words and heaven's visitation convict him. (The MESSENGER departs.)

CHORUS (singing) Ah! Cypris, thine the hand that guides the stubborn hearts of gods and men; thine, and that attendant boy's, who, with painted plumage gay, flutters round his victims on lightning wing. O'er the land and booming deep on golden pinion borne flits the god of Love, maddening the heart and beguiling the senses of all whom he attacks, savage whelps on mountains bred, ocean's monsters, creatures of this sun-warmed earth, and man; thine, O Cypris, thine alone the sovereign power to rule them all. (ARTEMIS appears above.)

ARTEMIS (chanting) Hearken, I bid thee, noble son of Aegeus: lo! 'tis I, Latona's child, that speak, I, Artemis. Why, Theseus, to thy sorrow dost thou rejoice at these tidings, seeing that thou hast slain thy son most impiously, listening to a charge not clearly proved, but falsely sworn to by thy wife? though clearly has the curse therefrom upon thee fallen. Why dost thou not for very shame hide beneath the dark places of the earth, or change thy human life and soar on wings to escape this tribulation? 'Mongst men of honour thou hast now no share in life. (She now speaks.) Hearken, Theseus; I will put thy wretched case. Yet will it naught avail thee, if I do, but vex thy heart; still with this intent I came, to show thy son's pure heart,-that he may die with honour,-as well the frenzy and, in a sense, the nobleness of thy wife; for she was cruelly stung with a passion for thy son by that goddess whom all we, that joy in virgin purity, detest. And though she strove to conquer love by resolution, yet by no fault of hers she fell, thanks to her nurse's strategy, who did reveal her malady unto thy son under oath. But he would none of her counsels, as indeed was right, nor yet, when thou didst revile him, would he break the oath he swore, from piety. She meantime, fearful of being found out, wrote a lying letter, destroying by guile thy son, but yet persuading thee.

THESEUS Woe is me!

ARTEMIS Doth my story wound thee, Theseus? Be still awhile; hear what follows, so wilt thou have more cause to groan. Dost remember those three prayers thy father granted thee, fraught with certain issue? 'Tis one of these thou hast misused, unnatural wretch, against thy son, instead of aiming it at an enemy. Thy sea-god sire, 'tis true, for all his kind intent, hath granted that boon he was compelled, by reason of his promise, to grant. But thou alike in his eyes and in mine hast shewn thy evil heart, in that thou hast forestalled all proof or voice prophetic, hast made no inquiry, nor taken time for consideration, but with undue haste cursed thy son even to the death.

THESEUS Perdition seize me! Queen revered!

ARTEMIS An awful deed was thine, but still even for this thou mayest obtain pardon; for it was Cypris that would have it so, sating the fury of her soul. For this is law amongst us gods; none of us will thwart his neighbour's will, but ever we stand aloof. For be well assured, did I not fear Zeus, never would I have incurred the bitter shame of handing over to death a man of all his kind to me most dear. As for thy sin, first thy ignorance absolves thee from its villainy, next thy wife, who is dead, was lavish in her use of convincing arguments to influence thy mind. On thee in chief this storm of woe hath burst, yet is it some grief to me as well; for when the righteous die, there is no joy in heaven, albeit we try to destroy the wicked, house and home.

CHORUS (chanting) Lo! where he comes, this hapless youth, his fair young flesh and auburn locks most shamefully handled. Unhappy house! what two-fold sorrow doth o'ertake its halls, through heaven's ordinance! (HIPPOLYTUS enters, assisted by his attendants.)

HIPPOLYTUS (chanting) Ah! ah! woe is me! foully undone by an impious father's impious imprecation! Undone, undone! woe is me! Through my head dart fearful pains; my brain throbs convulsively. Stop, let me rest my worn-out frame. Oh, oh! Accursed steeds, that mine own hand did feed, ye have been my ruin and my death. O by the gods, good sirs, beseech ye, softly touch my wounded limbs. Who stands there at my right side? Lift me tenderly; with slow and even step conduct a poor wretch cursed by his mistaken sire. Great Zeus, dost thou see this? Me thy reverent worshipper, me who left all men behind in purity, plunged thus into yawning Hades 'neath the earth, reft of life; in vain the toils I have endured through my piety towards mankind. Ah me! ah me! O the thrill of anguish shooting through me! Set me down, poor wretch I am; come Death to set me free! Kill me, end my sufferings. O for a sword two-edged to hack my flesh, and close this mortal life! Ill-fated curse of my father! the crimes of bloody kinsmen, ancestors of old, now pass their boundaries and tarry not, and upon me are they come all guiltless as I am; ah! why? Alas, alas! what can I say? How from my life get rid of this relentless agony? O that the stern Death-god, night's black visitant, would give my sufferings rest!

ARTEMIS Poor sufferer! cruel the fate that links thee to it! Thy noble soul hath been thy ruin.

HIPPOLYTUS Ah! the fragrance from my goddess wafted! Even in my agony I feel thee near and find relief; she is here in this very place, my goddess Artemis.

ARTEMIS She is, poor sufferer! the goddess thou hast loved the best.

HIPPOLYTUS Dost see me, mistress mine? dost see my present suffering?

ARTEMIS I see thee, but mine eyes no tear may weep.

HIPPOLYTUS Thou hast none now to lead the hunt or tend thy fane.

ARTEMIS None now; yet e'en in death I love thee still.

HIPPOLYTUS None to groom thy steeds, or guard thy

shrines.

ARTEMIS 'Twas Cypris, mistress of iniquity, devised this evil.

HIPPOLYTUS Ah me! now know I the goddess who destroyed me.

ARTEMIS She was jealous of her slighted honour, vexed at thy chaste life.

HIPPOLYTUS Ah! then I see her single hand hath struck down three of us.

ARTEMIS Thy sire and thee, and last thy father's wife.

HIPPOLYTUS My sire's ill-luck as well as mine I mourn.

ARTEMIS He was deceived by a goddess's design.

HIPPOLYTUS Woe is thee, my father, in this sad mischance!

THESEUS My son, I am a ruined man; life has no joys for me.

HIPPOLYTUS For this mistake I mourn thee rather than myself.

THESEUS O that I had died for thee, my son!

HIPPOLYTUS Ah! those fatal gifts thy sire Poseidon gave.

THESEUS Would God these lips had never uttered that prayer!

HIPPOLYTUS Why not? thou wouldst in any case have slain me in thy fury then.

THESEUS Yes; Heaven had perverted my power to think.

HIPPOLYTUS O that the race of men could bring a curse upon the gods!

ARTEMIS Enough! for though thou pass to gloom beneath the earth, the wrath of Cypris shall not, at her will, fall on thee unrequited, because thout hadst a noble righteous soul. For I with mine own hand will with these unerring shafts avenge me on another, who is her votary, dearest to her of all the sons of men. And to thee, poor sufferer, for thy anguish now will grant high honours in the city of Troezen; for thee shall maids unwed before their marriage cut off their hair, thy harvest through the long roll of time of countless bitter tears. Yea, and for ever shall the virgin choir hymn thy sad memory, nor shall Phaedra's love for thee fall into oblivion and pass away unnoticed. But thou, O son of old Aegeus, take thy son in thine arms, draw him close to thee, for unwittingly thou slewest him, and men may well commit an error when gods put it in their way. And thee Hippolytus, I admonish; hate not thy sire, for in this death thou dost but meet thy destined fate. And now farewell! 'tis not for me to gaze upon the dead, or pollute my sight with death-scenes, and e'en now I see thee nigh that evil. (ARTEMIS vanishes.)

HIPPOLYTUS Farewell, blest virgin queen! leave me now! Easily thou resignest our long friendship! I am reconciled with my father at thy desire, yea, for ever before I would obey thy bidding. Ah me! the darkness is settling even now upon my eyes. Take me, father, in thy arms, lift me up.

THESEUS Woe is me, my son! what art thou doing to me thy hapless sire!

HIPPOLYTUS I am a broken man; yes, I see the gates that close upon the dead.

THESEUS Canst leave me thus with murder on my soul!

HIPPOLYTUS No, no; I set thee free from this bloodguiltiness.

THESEUS What sayest thou? dost absolve me from bloodshed?

HIPPOLYTUS Artemis, the archer-queen, is my witness

that I do.

THESEUS My own dear child, how generous dost thou show thyself to thy father!

HIPPOLYTUS Farewell, dear father! a long farewell to thee!

THESEUS O that holy, noble soul of thine!

HIPPOLYTUS Pray to have children such as me born in lawful wedlock.

THESEUS O leave me not, my son; endure awhile.

HIPPOLYTUS 'Tis finished, my endurance; I die, father; quickly veil my face with a mantle.

THESEUS O glorious Athens, realm of Pallas, what a splendid hero ye have lost! Ah me, ah me! How oft shall I remember thy evil works, P Cypris!

CHORUS (singing) On all our citizens hath come this universal sorrow, unforeseen. Now shall the copious tear gush forth, for sad news about great men takes more than usual hold upon the heart.

THE END

Heracles

Dramatis Personae

AMPHITRYON, husband of Alcmena, the mother of HERACLES
MEGARA, wife of HERACLES, daughter of Creon
LYCUS, unlawful King of Thebes
IRIS
MADNESS
MESSENGER
HERACLES, son of Zeus and Alcmena
THESEUS, King of Athens
CHORUS OF OLD MEN OF THEBES

Before the palace of HERACLES at Thebes. Nearby stands the altar of Zeus, on the steps of which are now seated AMPHITRYON, MEGARA and her sons by HERACLES. They are seeking refuge at the altar.

AMPHITRYON What mortal hath not heard of him who shared a wife with Zeus, Amphitryon of Argos, whom on a day Alcaeus, son of Perseus begat, Amphitryon the father of Heracles? He it was dwelt here in Thebes, where from the sowing of the dragon's teeth grew up a crop of earthborn giants; for of these Ares saved a scanty band, and their children's children people the city of Cadmus. Hence sprung

Creon, son of Menoeceus, king of this land; and Creon became the father of this lady Megara, whom once all Cadmus' race escorted with the glad music of lutes at her wedding, in the day that Heracles, illustrious chief, led her to my halls. Now he, my son, left Thebes where I was settled, left his wife Megara and her kin, eager to make his home in Argolis, in that walled town which the Cyclopes built, whence I am exiled for the slaying of Electryon; so he, wishing to lighten my affliction and to find a home in his own land, did offer Eurystheus a mighty price for my recall, even to free the world of savage monsters, whether it was that Hera goaded him to submit to this, or that fate was leagued against him. Divers are the toils he hath accomplished, and last of all hath he passed through the mouth of Taenarus into the halls of Hades to drag to the light that hound with bodies three, and thence is he never returned. Now there is an ancient legend amongst the race of Cadmus, that one Lycus in days gone by was husband to Dirce being king of this city with its seven towers, before that Amphion and Zethus, sons of Zeus, lords of the milk-white steeds, became rulers in the land. His son, called by the same name as his father, albeit no Theban but a stranger from Euboea, slew Creon, and after that seized the government, having fallen on this city when weakened by dissension. So this connection with Creon is likely to prove to us a serious evil; for now that my son is in the bowels of the earth, this illustrious monarch Lycus is bent on extirpating the children of Heracles, to quench one bloody feud with another, likewise his wife and me, if useless age like mine is to rank amongst men, that the boys may never grow up to exact a blood-penalty of their uncle's family. So I, left here by my son, whilst he is gone into the pitchy darkness of the earth, to tend and guard his children in his house, am taking my place with their mother, that the race of Heracles may not perish, here at the altar of Zeus the Saviour, which my own gallant child set up to commemorate his glorious victory over the Minyae. And here we are careful to keep our station, though in need of everything, of food, of drink, and raiment, huddled together on the hard bare ground; for we are barred out from our house and sit here for want of any other safety.

As for friends, some I see are insincere; while others, who are staunch, have no power to help us further. This is what misfortune means to man; God grant it may never fall to the lot of any who bears the least goodwill to me, to apply this never-failing test of friendship!

MEGARA Old warrior, who erst did raze the citadel of the Taphians leading on the troops of Thebes to glory, how uncertain are God's dealings with man! For I, as far as concerned my sire was never an outcast of fortune, for he was once accounted a man of might by reason of his wealth, possessed as he was of royal power, for which long spears are launched at the lives of the fortunate through love of it; children too he had; and me did he betroth to thy son, matching me in glorious marriage with Heracles. Whereas now all that is dead and gone from us; and I and thou, old friend, art doomed to die, and these children of Heracles, whom I am guarding 'neath my wing as a bird keepeth her tender chicks under her. And they the while in turn keep asking me, "Mother, whither is our father gone from the land? what is he about? when will he return?" Thus they inquire for their father, in childish perplexity; while I put them off with excuses, inventing stories; but still I wonder if 'tis he whenever a door creaks on its hinges, and up they all start, thinking to embrace their father's knees. What hope or way of salvation art thou now devising, old friend? for to thee I look. We can never steal beyond the boundaries of the land unseen, for there is too strict a watch set on us at every outlet, nor have we any longer hopes of safety in our friends. Whatever thy scheme is, declare it, lest our death be made ready, while we are only prolonging the time, powerless to escape.

AMPHITRYON 'Tis by no means easy, my daughter, to give one's earnest advice on such matters easily, without weary thought.

MEGARA Dost need a further taste of grief, or cling so fast to life?

AMPHITRYON Yes, I love this life, and cling to its hopes.

MEGARA So do I; but it boots not to expect the unexpected, old friend.

AMPHITRYON In these delays is left the only cure for our evils.

MEGARA 'Tis the pain of that interval I feel so.

AMPHITRYON Daughter, there may yet be a happy escape from present troubles for me and thee; my son, thy husband, may yet arrive. So calm thyself, and wipe those tears from thy children's eyes, and soothe them with soft words, inventing a tale to delude them, piteous though such fraud be. Yea, for men's misfortunes ofttimes flag, and the stormy wind doth not always blow so strong, nor are the prosperous ever so; for all things change, making way for each other. The bravest man is he who relieth ever on his hopes, but despair is the mark of a coward. (The CHORUS OF OLD MEN OF THEBES enters.)

CHORUS (chanting, strophe)

To the sheltering roof, to the old man's couch, leaning on my staff have I set forth, chanting a plaintive dirge like some bird grown grey, I that am but a voice and nothing more, a fancy bred of the visions of sleep by night, palsied with age, yet meaning kindly. All hail! ye orphaned babes! all hail, old friend thou too, -unhappy mother, wailing for thy husband in the halls of Hades!

(antistrophe)

Faint not too soon upon your way, nor let your limbs grow weary, even as a colt beneath the yoke grows weary as he mounts some stony hill, dragging the weight of a wheeled car. Take hold of hand or robe, whoso feels his footsteps falter. Old friend, escort another like thyself, who erst amid his toiling peers in the days of our youth would take his place beside thee, no blot upon his country's glorious record.

See, how like their father's sternly flash these children's eyes! Misfortune, God wot, hath not failed his children, nor yet hath his comeliness been denied them. O Hellas! if thou lose these, of what allies wilt thou rob thyself!

LEADER OF THE CHORUS But I see Lycus, the ruler of this land, drawing near the house. (Lycus and his attendants enter.)

LYCUS One question, if I may, to this father of Heracles and his wife; and certainly as your lord and master I have a right to put what questions choose. How long do ye seek to prolong your lives? What hope, what succour do ye see to save you from death? Do you trust that these children's father, who lies dead in the halls of Hades, will return? How unworthily ye show your sorrow at having to die, thou (to AMPHITRYON) after thy idle boasts, scattered broadcast through Hellas, that Zeus was partner in thy marriage-bed and there begat a new god; and thou (to MEGARA) after calling thyself the wife of so peerless a lord.

After all, what was the fine exploit thy husband achieved, if he did kil a hydra in a marsh or that monster of Nemea? which he caught in a snare, for all he says he strangled it to death in his arms. Are these your weapons for the hard struggle? Is it for this then that Heracles' children should be spared? a man who has won a reputation for valour in his contests with beasts, in all else a weakling; who ne'er buckled shield to arm nor faced the spear, but with a bow, that coward's weapon, was ever ready to run away. Archery is no test of manly bravery; no! he is a man who keeps his post in the ranks and steadily faces the swift wound the spear may plough. My policy, again, old man, shows no reckless cruelty, but caution; for I am well aware I slew Creon, the father of Megara, and am in possession of his throne. So I have no wish that these children should grow up and be left to take vengeance on me in requital for what I have done.

AMPHITRYON As for Zeus, let Zeus defend his son's case; but as for me, Heracles, I am only anxious on thy behalf to prove by what I say this tyrant's ignorance; for I cannot allow thee to be ill spoken of. First then for that which should never have been said,-for to speak of thee Heracles as coward is, methinks, outside the pale of speech,-of that must I clear the with heaven to witness. I appeal then to the thunder of Zeus, and the chariot wherein he rode, when he pierced the giants, earth's brood, to the heart with his winged shafts, and with gods uplifted the glorious triumph-song; or go to Pholoe and ask the insolent tribe of four-legged Centaurs, thou craven king, ask them who they would judge their bravest foe; will they not say my son, who according to thee is but a pretender? Wert thou to ask Euboean Dirphys, thy native place, it would nowise sing thy praise, for thou hast never done a single gallant deed to which thy country can witness. Next thou dost disparage that clever invention, an archer's weapon; come, listen to me and learn wisdom. A man who fights in line is a slave to his weapons, and if his fellow-comrades want for courage he is slain himself through the cowardice of his neighbours, or, if he break his spear, he has not wherewithal to defend his body from death, having only one means of defence; whereas all who are armed with the trusty bow, though they have but one weapon, yet is it the best; for a man, after discharging countless arrows, still has others wherewith to defend himself from death, and standing at a distance keeps off the enemy, wounding them for all their watchfulness with shafts invisible, and never exposing himself to the foe, but keeping under cover; and this is far the wisest course in battle, to harm the enemy, if they are not stationed out of shot, and keep safe oneself. These arguments are completely opposite to thine with regard to the point at issue. Next, why art thou desirous of slaying these children? What have they done to thee? One piece of wisdom credit thee with, thy coward terror of a brave man's descendants. Still it is hard on us, if for thy cowardice we must die; a fate that ought to have overtaken thee at our braver hands, if Zeus had been fairly disposed towards us. But, if thou art so anxious to make thyself supreme in the land, let us at least go into exile; abstain from all violence, else thou wilt suffer by it whenso the deity causes fortune's breeze to veer round.

Ah! thou land of Cadmus,-for to thee too will I turn, upbraiding thee with words of reproach,-is this your succour of Heracles and his children? the man who faced alone the Minyan host in battle and allowed Thebes to see the light with freemen's eyes. I cannot praise Hellas, nor will I ever keep silence, finding her so craven as regards my son; she should have come with fire and sword and warrior's arms to help these tender babes, to requite him for all his labours in purging land and sea. Such help, my children, neither Hellas nor the city of Thebes affords you; to me a feeble friend ye look, that am but empty sound and nothing more. For the vigour which once I had, is gone from me; my limbs are palsied with age, and my strength is decayed. Were I but young and still a man of my hands, I would have seized my spear and dabbled those flaxen locks of his with blood, so that the coward would now be flying from my prowes beyond the bounds of Atlas.

LEADER Have not the brave amongst mankind a fair opening for speech, albeit slow to begin?

LYCUS Say what thou wilt of me in thy exalted phrase, but I by deeds will make thee rue those words. (Calling to his servants) Ho! bid wood-cutters go, some to Helicon, others to the glens of Parnassus, and cut me logs of oak, and when they are brought to the town, pile up a stack of wood all round the altar on either side thereof, and set fire to it and burn them all alive, that they may learn that the dead no longer rules this land, but that for the present I am king. (angrily to the CHORUS) As for you, old men, since ye thwart my views, not for the children of Heracles alone shall ye lament but likewise for every blow that strikes his house, and ye shall ne'er forget ye are slaves and I your prince.

LEADER Ye sons of Earth, whom Ares on a day did sow, when from the dragon's ravening jaw he had torn the teeth, up with your staves, whereon ye lean your hands, and dash out this miscreant's brains! a fellow who, without even being a Theban, but a foreigner, lords it shamefully o'er the younger folk; but my master shalt thou never be to thy joy, nor shalt thou reap the harvest of all my toil; begone with my curse upon thee! carry thy insolence back to the place whence it came. For never whilst I live, shalt thou slay these sons of Heracles; not so deep beneath the earth hath their father disappeared from his children's ken. Thou art in possession of this land which thou hast ruined, while he its benefactor has missed his just reward; and yet do I take too much upon myself because I help those I love after their death, when most they need a friend? Ah! right hand, how fain wouldst thou wield the spear, but thy weakness is a death-blow to thy fond desire; for then had I stopped thee calling me slave, and I would have governed Thebes, wherein thou art now exulting, with credit; for city sick with dissension and evil counsels thinketh not aright; otherwise it would never have accepted thee as its master.

MEGARA Old sirs, I thank you; 'tis right that friends should feel virtuous indignation on behalf of those they love; but do not on our account vent your anger on the tyrant to your own undoing. Hear my advice, Amphitryon, if haply there appear to thee to be aught in what I say. I love my children; strange if I did not love those whom I laboured to bring forth! Death I count a dreadful fate; but the man who wrestles with necessity I esteem a fool. Since we must die, let us do so without being burnt alive, to furnish our foes with food for merriment, which to my mind is an evil worse than death; for many a fair guerdon do we owe our family. Thine has ever been a warrior's fair fame, so 'tis not to be endured that thou shouldst die a coward's death; and my husband's reputation needs no one to witness that he would ne'er consent to save these children's lives by letting them incur the stain of cowardice; for the noble are afflicted by disgrace on account of their children, nor must I shrink from following my lord's example. As to thy hopes consider how I weigh them. Thou thinkest thy son will return from beneath the earth: who ever has come back from the dead out of the halls of Hades? Thou hast a hope perhaps of softening this man by entreaty: no, no! better to fly from one's enemy when he is so brutish, but yield to men of breeding and wisdom; for thou wilt more easily obtain mercy there by friendly overtures. True, a thought has already occurred to me that we might by entreaty obtain a sentence of exile for the children; yet this too is misery, to compass their deliverance with dire penury as the result; for 'tis a saying that hosts look sweetly on banished friends for a day and no more. Steel thy heart to die with us, for that awaits thee after all. By thy brave soul I challenge thee, old friend; for whoso struggles hard to escape destiny shows zeal no doubt, but 'tis zeal with a taint of folly; for what must be, no one will ever avail to alter.

LEADER If a man had insulted thee, while yet my arms were lusty, there would have been an easy way to stop him; but now am I a thing of naught; and so thou henceforth, Amphitryon, must scheme how to avert misfortune.

AMPHITRYON 'Tis not cowardice or any longing for life that hinders my dying, but my wish to save my son's children, though no doubt I am vainly wishing for impossibilities. Lo! here is my neck ready for thy sword to pierce, my body for thee to hack or hurl from the rock; only one boon I crave for both of us, O king; slay me and this hapless mother before thou slay the children, that we may not see the hideous sight, as they gasp out their lives, calling on their mother and their father's sire; for the rest work thy will, if so thou art inclined; for we have no defence against death.

MEGARA I too implore thee add a second boon, that by thy single act thou mayst put us both under a double obligation; suffer me to deck my children in the robes of death,-first opening the palace gates, for now are we shut out,-that this at least they may obtain from their father's halls.

LYCUS I grant it, and bid my servants undo the bolts. Go in and deck yourselves; robes I grudge not. But soon as ye have clothed yourselves, I will return to you to consign you to the nether world. (Lycus and his retinue withdraw.)

MEGARA Children, follow the footsteps of your hapless mother to your father's halls, where others possess his substance, though his name is still ours. (MEGARA and her children enter the palace.)

AMPHITRYON O Zeus, in vain it seems, did I get thee to share my bride with me; in vain used we to call thee father of my son. After all thou art less our friend than thou didst pretend. Great god as thou art, I, a mere mortal. surpass thee in true worth. For I did not betray the children of Heracles; but thou by stealth didst find thy way to my couch, taking another's wife without leave given, while to save thy own friends thou hast no skill. Either thou art a god of little sense, or else naturally unjust. (AMPHITRYON follows MEGARA into the palace.)

CHORUS (singing, strophe 1)

Phoebus is singing a plaintive dirge to drown his happier strains, striking with key of gold his sweet-tongued lyre; so too am I fain to sing a song of praise, a crown to all his toil, concerning him who is gone to the gloom beneath the nether world, whether I am to call him son of Zeus or of Amphitryon. For the praise of noble toils accomplished is a glory to the dead. First he cleared the grove of Zeus of a lion, and put its skin upon his back, hiding his auburn hair in its fearful gaping jaws;

(antistrophe 1)

Then on a day, with murderous bow he wounded the race of wild Centaurs, that range the hills, slaying them with winged shafts; Peneus, the river of fair eddies, knows him well, and those far fields unharvested, and the steadings on Pelion and they who haunt the glens of Homole bordering thereupon, whence they rode forth to conquer Thessaly, arming themselves with pines for clubs; likewise he slew that dappled hind with horns of gold, that preyed upon the country-folk, glorifying Artemis, huntress queen of Oenoe;

(strophe 2)

Next he mounted on a car and tamed with the bit the steeds of Diomede, that greedily champed their bloody food at gory mangers with jaws unbridled, devouring with hideous joy the flesh of men; then crossing Hebrus' silver stream he still toiled on to perform the hests of the tyrant of Mycenae, till he came to the strand of the Malian gulf by the streams of Anaurus, where he slew with his arrows Cycnus, murderer of his guests, the savage wretch who dwelt in Amphanae;

(antistrophe 2)

Also he came to those minstrel maids, to their orchard

in the west, to pluck from the leafy apple-tree its golden fruit, when he had slain the tawny dragon, whose awful coils were twined all round to guard it; and he made his way into ocean's lairs, bringing calm to men that use the oar; moreover he sought the home of Atlas, and stretched out his hands to uphold the firmament, and on his manly shoulders took the starry mansions of the gods;

(strophe 3)

Then he went through the waves of heaving Euxine against the mounted host of Amazons dwelling round Maeotis, the lake that is fed by many a stream, having gathered to his standard all his friends from Hellas, to fetch the gold-embroidered raiment of the warrior queen, a deadly quest for a girdle. And Hellas won those glorious spoils of the barbarian maid, and safe in Mycenae are they now. On Lerna's murderous hound, the many-headed hydra, he set his branding-iron, and smeared its venom on his darts, wherewith he slew the shepherd of Erytheia, a monster with three bodies;

(antistrophe 3)

And many another glorious achievement he brought to a happy issue; to Hades' house of tears hath he now sailed, the goal of his labours, where he is ending his career of toil, nor cometh he thence again. Now is thy house left without a friend, and Charon's boat awaits thy children to bear them on that journey out of life, whence is no returning, contrary to God's law and man's justice; and it is to thy prowess that thy house is looking although thou art not here. Had I been strong and lusty, able to brandish the spear in battle's onset, my Theban compeers too, I would have stood by thy children to champion them; but now my happy youth is gone and I am left.

But lo! I see the children of Heracles who was erst so great, clad in the vesture of the grave, and his loving wife dragging her babes along at her side, and that hero's aged sire. Ah! woe is me! no longer can I stem the flood of tears that spring to my old eyes. (MEGARA, AMPHITRYON, and the children enter from the palace.)

MEGARA Come now, who is to sacrifice or butcher these poor children? or rob me of my wretched life? Behold! the victims are ready to be led to Hades' halls. O my children! an ill-matched company are we hurried off to die, old men and babes, and mothers, all together. Alas! for my sad fate and my children's, whom these eyes now for the last time behold. So I gave you birth and reared you only for our foes to mock, to flout, and slay. Ah me! how bitterly my hopes have disappointed me in the expectation once formed from the words of your father. (Addressing each of her sons in turn) To thee thy dead sire was for giving Argos; and thou wert to dwell in the halls of Eurystheus, lording it o'er the fair fruitful land of Argolis; and o'er thy head would he throw that lion's skin wherewith himself was girt. Thou wert to be king of Thebes, famed for its chariots, receiving as thy heritage my broad lands, for so thou didst coax thy father dear; and to thy hand used he to resign the carved club, his sure defence, pretending to give it thee. To thee he promised to give Oechalia, which once his archery had wasted. Thus with three principalities would your father exalt you his three sons, proud of your manliness; while I was choosing the best brides for you, scheming to link you by marriage to Athens, Thebes, and Sparta, that ye might live a happy life with a fast sheet-anchor to hold by. And now that is all vanished; fortune's breeze hath veered and given to you for brides the maidens of death in their stead, and tears to me to bathe them in; woe is me for my foolish thoughts and your grandsire here is celebrating your marriage-feast, accepting Hades as the father of your brides, a grim relationship to make. Ah me! which of you shall I first press to my bosom, which last? on which bestow my kiss, or clasp close to me? Oh! would that like the bee with russet wing, I could collect from every source my sighs in one, and, blending them together, shed them in one copious flood! Heracles, dear husband mine, to thee I call, if haply mortal voice can make itself heard in Hades' halls; thy father and children are dying and I am doomed, I who once because of thee was counted blest as men count bliss. Come to our rescue; appear, I pray, if but as a phantom, since thy mere coming would be enough, for they are cowards compared with thee, who are slaying thy children.

AMPHITRYON Lady, do thou prepare the funeral rites; but I, O Zeus, stretching out my hand to heaven, call on thee to help these children, if such be thy intention; for soon will any aid of thine be unavailing; and yet thou hast been oft invoked; my toil is wasted; death seems inevitable. Ye aged friends, the joys of life are few; so take heed that ye pass through it as gladly as ye may, without a thought of sorrow from morn till night; for time recks little of preserving our hopes; and, when he has busied himself on his own business, away he flies. Look at me, a man who had made mark amongst his fellows by deeds of note; yet hath fortune in a single day robbed me of it as of a feather that floats away toward the sky. know not any whose plenteous wealth and high reputation is fixed and sure; fare ye well, for now have ye seen the last of your old friend, my comrades. (MEGARA catches sight of HERACLES approaching.) MEGARA Ha! old friend, is it my own, my dearest I behold? or what am I to say?

AMPHITRYON I know not, my daughter; I too am struck dumb.

MEGARA Is this he who, they told us, was beneath the earth?

AMPHITRYON 'Tis he, unless some day-dream mocks our sight.

MEGARA What am I saying? What visions do these anxious eyes behold? Old man, this is none other than thy own son. Come hither, my children, cling to your father's robe, make haste to come, never loose your hold, for here is one to help you, nowise behind our saviour Zeus. (HERACLES enters.)

HERACLES All hail! my house, and portals of my home, how glad am I to emerge to the light and see thee. Ha! what is this? I see my children before the house in the garb of death, with chaplets on their heads, my wife amid a throng of men, and my father weeping o'er some mischance. Let me draw near to them and inquire; lady, what strange stroke of fate hath fallen on the house?

MEGARA Dearest of all mankind to me! O ray of light appearing to thy sire! art thou safe, and is thy coming just in time to help thy dear ones?

HERACLES What meanest thou? what is this confusion I find on my arrival, father?

MEGARA We are being ruined; forgive me, old friend, if I have anticipated that which thou hadst a right to tell him; for woman's nature is perhaps more prone than man's to grief, and they are my children that were being led to death, which was my own lot too.

HERACLES Great Apollo! what a prelude to thy story!

MEGARA Dead are my brethren, dead my hoary sire.

HERACLES How so? what befell him? who dealt the fatal blow?

MEGARA Lycus, our splendid monarch, slew him.

HERACLES Did he meet him in fair fight, or was the land sick and weak?

MEGARA Aye, from faction; now is he master of the city of Cadmus with its seven gates.

HERACLES Why hath panic fallen on thee and my aged sire?

MEGARA He meant to kill thy father, me, and my children.

HERACLES Why, what had he to fear from my orphan babes?

MEGARA He was afraid they might some day avenge Creon's death.

HERACLES What means this dress they wear, suited to

the dead?

MEGARA 'Tis the garb of death we have already put on.

HERACLES And were ye being haled to death? O woe is me!

MEGARA Yes, deserted by every friend, and informed that thou wert dead.

HERACLES What put such desperate thoughts into your heads?

MEGARA That was what the heralds of Eurystheus kept proclaiming.

HERACLES Why did ye leave my hearth and home?

MEGARA He forced us; thy father was dragged from his bed.

HERACLES Had he no mercy, to ill-use the old man so?

MEGARA Mercy forsooth! that goddess and he dwell far enough apart.

HERACLES Was I so poor in friends in my absence?

MEGARA Who are the friends of a man in misfortune?

HERACLES Do they make so light of my hard warring with the Minyae?

MEGARA Misfortune, to repeat it to thee, has no friends.

HERACLES Cast from your heads these chaplets of death, look up to the light, for instead of the nether gloom your eyes behold the welcome sun. I, meantime, since here is work for my hand, will first go raze this upstart tyrant's halls, and when I have beheaded the miscreant, I will throw him to dogs to tear; and every Theban who I find has played the traitor after my kindness, will I destroy with this victorious club; the rest will I scatter with my feathered shafts and fill Ismenus full of bloody corpses, and Dirce's clear fount shall run red with gore. For whom ought I to help rather than wife and children and aged sire? Farewell my labours! for it was in vain I accomplished them rather than succoured these. And yet I ought to die in their defence, since they for their sire were doomed; else what shall we find so noble in having fought a hydra and a lion at the hests of Eurystheus, if I make no effort to save my own children from death? No longer I trow, as heretofore, shall I be called Heracles the victor.

LEADER OF THE CHORUS 'Tis only right that parents should help their children, their aged sires, and the partners of their marriage.

AMPHITRYON My son, 'tis like thee to show thy love for thy dear ones and thy hate for all that is hostile; only curb excessive hastiness.

HERACLES Wherein, father, am I now showing more than fitting haste?

AMPHITRYON The king hath a host of allies, needy villains though pretending to be rich, who sowed dissension and o'erthrew the state with a view to plundering their neighbours; for the wealth they had in their houses was ali spent, dissipated by their sloth. Thou wast seen entering the city; and, that being so, beware that thou bring not thy enemies together and be slain unawares.

HERACLES Little I reck if the whole city saw me; but chancing to see a bird perched in an ill-omened spot, from it I learnt that some trouble had befallen my house; so I purposely made my entry to the land by stealth.

AMPHITRYON For thy lucky coming hither, go salute thy household altar, and let thy father's halls behold thy face. For soon will the king be here in person to drag away thy wife and children and murder them, and to add me to the bloody list. But if thou remain on the spot all will go well, and thou wilt profit by this security; but do not rouse thy city ere thou hast these matters well in train, my son.

HERACLES I will do so; thy advice is good; I will enter my house. After my return at length from the sunless den of Hades and the maiden queen of hell, I will not neglect to greet first of all the gods beneath my roof.

AMPHITRYON Why, didst thou in very deed go to the house of Hades, my son?

HERACLES Aye, and brought to the light that three-headed monster.

AMPHITRYON Didst worst him in fight, or receive him from the goddess?

HERACLES In fair fight; for I had been lucky enough to witness the rites of the initiated.

AMPHITRYON Is the monster really lodged in the house of Eurystheus?

HERACLES The grove of Demeter and the city of Hermione are his prison.

AMPHITRYON Does not Eurystheus know that thou hast returned to the upper world?

HERACLES He knows not; I came hither first to learn your news.

AMPHITRYON How is it thou wert so long beneath the earth?

HERACLES I stayed awhile attempting to bring back Theseus from Hades, father.

AMPHITRYON Where is he? gone to his native land?

HERACLES He set out for Athens right glad to have escaped from the lower world. Come, children, attend your father to the house. My entering in is fairer in your eyes, I trow, than my going out. Take heart, and no more let the tears stream from your eyes; thou too, dear wife, collect thy courage, cease from fear; let go my robe; for I cannot fly away, nor have I any wish to flee from those I love. Ah! they do not loose their hold, but cling to my garments all the more; were ye in such jeopardy? Well, I must lead them, taking them by the hand to draw them after me, like a ship when towing; for I too do not reject the care of my children; here all mankind are equal; all love their children, both those of high estate and those; who are naught; 'tis wealth that makes distinctions among them; some have, others want; but all the human race loves its offspring. (HERACLES, MEGARA, AMPHITRYON and the children enter the palace.)

CHORUS (singing, strophe 1)

Dear to me is youth, but old age is ever hanging o'er my head, a burden heavier than Aetna's crags, casting its pall of gloom upon my eyes. Oh! never may the wealth of Asia's kings tempt me to barter for houses stored with gold my happy youth, which is in wealth and poverty alike most fair! But old age is gloomy and deathly; I hate it; let it sink beneath the waves! Would it had never found its way to the homes and towns of mortal men, but were still drifting on for ever down the wind.

(antistrophe 1)

Had the gods shown discernment and wisdom, as mortals count these things, men would have gotten youth twice over, a visible mark of worth amongst whomsoever found, and after death would these have retraced their steps once more to the sun-light, while the mean man would have had but a single portion of life; and thus would it have been possible to distinguish the good and the bad, just as sailors know the number of the stars amid the clouds. But, as it is, the gods have set no certain boundary 'twixt good and bad, but time's onward roll brings increase only to man's wealth.

(strophe 2)

Never will I cease to link in one the Graces and the Muses, fairest union. Never may my lines be cast among untutored boors, but ever may I find a place among the crowned choir! Yes, still the aged bard lifts up his voice of bygone memories; still is my song of the triumphs of Heracles, whether Bromius the giver of wine is nigh, or the strains of the seven-stringed lyre and the Libyan flute are rising; not yet will I cease to sing the Muses' praise, my patrons in the dance.

(antistrophe 2)

As the maids of Delos raise their song of joy, circling round the temple gates in honour of Leto's fair son, the graceful dancer; so with my old lips will sing songs of victory at thy palace-doors, song of my old age, such as sings the dying swan; for there is a goodly theme for minstrelsy; he is the son of Zeus; yet high above his noble birth tower his deeds of prowess, for his toil secured this life of calm for man, having destroyed all fearsome beasts. (AMPHITRYON comes out of the palace as Lycus and his retinue enter.)

LYCUS Ha! Amphitryon, 'tis high time thou camest forth from the palace; ye have been too long arraying yourselves in the robes and trappings of the dead. Come, bid the wife and children of Heracles show themselves outside the house, to die on the conditions you yourselves offered.

AMPHITRYON O king, thou dost persecute me in my misery and heapest insult upon me over and above the loss of my son; thou shouldst have been more moderate in thy zeal, though thou art my lord and master. But since thou dost impose death's stern necessity on me, needs must I acquiesce and do thy will.

LYCUS Pray, where is Megara? where are the children of Alcmena's son?

AMPHITRYON She, I believe, so far as I can guess from outside-

LYCUS What grounds hast thou to base thy fancy on?

AMPHITRYON Is sitting as a suppliant on the altar's hallowed steps.

LYCUS Imploring them quite uselessly to save her life.

AMPHITRYON And calling on her dead husband, quite

in vain.

LYCUS He is nowhere near, and he certainly will never come.

AMPHITRYON No, unless perhaps a god should raise him from the dead.

LYCUS Go to her and bring her from the palace.

AMPHITRYON By doing so I should become an accomplice in her murder.

LYCUS Since thou hast this scruple, I, who have left fear behind, will myself bring out the mother and her children. Follow me, servants, that we may put an end to this delay of our work to our joy. (Lycus and his servants enter the palace.)

AMPHITRYON Then go thy way along the path of fate; for what remains, maybe another will provide. Expect for thy evil deeds to find some ill thyself. Ah! my aged friends, he is marching fairly to his doom; soon will he be entangled in the snare of the sword, thinking to slay his neighbours, the villain! I will hence, to see him fall dead; for the sight of a foe being slain and paying the penalty of his misdeeds gives pleasure. (AMPHITRYON follows Lycus into the palace.)

CHORUS (singing) Evil has changed sides; he who was erst a mighty king is now turning his life backward into the road to Hades.

Hail to thee! justice and heavenly retribution. At last hast thou reached the goal where thy death will pay the forfeit,

For thy insults against thy betters. Joy makes my tears burst forth. There is come a retribution, which the prince of the land never once thought in his heart would happen.

Come, old friends, let us look within to see if one we know has met the fate I hope.

LYCUS (within) Ah me! ah me!

CHORUS (singing) Ha! how sweet to hear that opening note of his within the house; death is not far off him now.

Hark! the prince cries out in his agony; that preludes death.

LYCUS (within) O kingdom of Cadmus, by treachery I am perishing!

CHORUS (singing) Thou wert thyself for making others perish; endure thy retribution; 'tis only the penalty of thy own deeds thou art paying.

Who was he, weak son of man, that aimed his silly saying at the blessed gods of heaven with impious blasphemy, maintaining that they are weaklings after all?

Old friends, our godless foe is now no more. The house is still; let us to our dancing. Yea, for fortune smiles upon my friends as I desire.

(strophe 1)

Dances and banquets now prevail throughout the holy town of Thebes. For release from tears and respite from sorrow give birth to song. The upstart king is dead and gone; our former monarch now is prince, having made his way even from the bourn of Acheron. Hope beyond all expectation is fulfilled.

(antistrophe 1)

To heed the right and wrong is heaven's care. 'Tis their gold and their good luck that lead men's hearts astray, bringing in their train unholy tyranny. For no man ever had the courage to reflect what reverses time might bring; but, disregarding law to gratify lawlessness, he shatters in gloom the car of happiness.

(strophe 2)

Deck thee with garlands, O Ismenus! break forth into dancing, ye paved streets of our seven-gated city! come Dirce, fount of waters fair; and joined with her ye daughters of Asopus, come from your father's waves to add your maiden voices to our hymn, the victor's prize that Heracles hath won. O Pythian rock, with forests crowned, and haunts of the Muses on Helicon! make my city and her walls re-echo with cries of joy; where sprang the earth-born crop to view, a warrior-host with shields of brass, who are handing on their realm to children's children, a light divine to Thebes.

(antistrophe 2)

All hail the marriage! wherein two bridegrooms shared; the one, a mortal; the other, Zeus, who came to wed the maiden sprung from Perseus; for that marriage of thine, O Zeus, in days gone by has been proved to me a true story beyond all expectation; and time hath shown the lustre of Heracles' prowess, who emerged from caverns 'neath the earth after leaving Pluto's halls below. To me art thou a worthier lord than that base-born king, who now lets it be plainly seen in this struggle 'twixt armed warriors, whether justice still finds favour in heaven. (The spectres of MADNESS and IRIS appear from above. The CHORUS sees them.) Ha! see there, my old comrades! is the same wild panic fallen on us all; what phantom is this I see hovering o'er the house? Fly, fly, bestir thy tardy steps! begone! away! away! O saviour prince, avert calamity from me!

IRIS Courage, old men! she, whom you see, is Madness, daughter of Night, and I am Iris, the handmaid of the gods. We have not come to do your city any hurt, but against the house of one man only is our warfare, even against him whom they call the son of Zeus and Alcmena. For until he had finished all his grievous toils, Destiny was preserving him, nor would father Zeus ever suffer me or Hera to harm him. But now that he hath accomplished the labours of Eurystheus, Hera is minded to brand him with the guilt of shedding kindred blood by slaying his own children, and I am one with her. Come then, maid unwed, child of murky Night, harden thy heart relentlessly, send forth frenzy upon him, confound his mind even to the slaying of his children, drive him, goad him wildly on his mad career, shake out the sails of death, that when he has sent o'er Acheron's ferry that fair group of children by his own murderous hand, he may learn to know how fiercely against him the wrath of Hera burns and may also experience mine; otherwise, if he escape punishment, the gods will become as naught, while man's power will grow.

MADNESS Of noble parents was I born, the daughter of Night, sprung from the blood of Uranus; and these prerogatives I hold, not to use them in anger against friends, nor have I any joy in visiting the homes of men; and fain would I counsel Hera, before I see her err, and thee too, if ye will hearken to my words. This man, against whose house thou art sending me, has made himself a name alike in heaven and earth; for, after taming pathless wilds and raging sea, he by his single might raised up again the honours of the gods when sinking before man's impiety; wherefore I counsel thee, do not wish him dire mishaps.

IRIS Spare us thy advice on Hera's and my schemes.

MADNESS I seek to turn thy steps into the best path instead of into this one of evil.

IRIS 'Twas not to practice self-control that the wife of Zeus sent thee hither.

MADNESS I call the sun-god to witness that herein I am acting against my will; but if indeed I must forthwith serve thee and Hera and follow you in full cry as hounds follow the huntsman, why go I will; nor shall ocean with its moaning waves, nor the earthquake, nor the thunderbolt with blast of agony be half so furious as the headlong rush I will make into the breast of Heracles; through his roof will I burst my way and swoop upon his house, after first slaying his children; nor shall their murderer know that he is killing his own-begotten babes, till he is released from my madness. Behold him! see how even now he is wildly tossing his head at the outset, and rolling his eyes fiercely from side to side without word; nor can he control his panting breath; but like a bull in act to charge, he bellows fearfully, calling on the goddesses of nether hell. Soon will I rouse thee to yet wilder dancing and sound a note of terror in thine ear. Soar away, O Iris, to Olympus on thy honoured course; while I unseen will steal into the halls of Heracles. (IRIS and MADNESS vanish.)

CHORUS (chanting) Alas! alas! lament, O city; the son of Zeus, thy fairest bloom, is being cut down.

Woe is thee, Hellas! that wilt cast from thee thy benefactor, and destroy him as he madly, wildly dances where no pipe is heard.

She is mounted on her car, the queen of sorrow and sighing, and is goading on her steeds, as if for outrage, the Gorgon child of Night, with hundred hissing serpent-heads, Madness of the flashing eyes.

Soon hath the god changed his good fortune; soon will his children breathe their last, slain by a father's hand.

Ah me! alas! soon will vengeance, mad, relentless, lay low by cruel death thy unhappy son, O Zeus, exacting a full penalty.

Alas, O house! the fiend begins her dance of death without the cymbal's crash, with no glad waving of the wine-god's staff.

Woe to these halls toward bloodshed she moves, and not to pour libations of the juice of the grape.

O children, haste to fly; that is the chant of death her piping plays.

Ah, yes! he is chasing the children. Never, ah! never will Madness lead her revel rout in vain.

Ah misery! Ah me! how I lament that aged sire, that mother too that bore his babes in vain.

Look! look! A tempest rocks the house; the roof is falling with it. Oh! what art thou doing, son of Zeus? Thou art sending hell's confusion against thy house, as erst did Pallas on Enceladus. (A MESSENGER enters from the palace.)

MESSENGER Ye hoary men of eld!

CHORUS Why, oh! why this loud address to me?

MESSENGER Awful is the sight within!

CHORUS No need for me to call another to announce that.

MESSENGER Dead lie the children.

CHORUS Alas!

MESSENGER Ah weep! for here is cause for weeping.

CHORUS A cruel murder, wrought by parents' hands!

MESSENGER No words can utter more than we have suffered.

CHORUS What, canst thou prove this piteous ruin was a father's outrage on his children? Tell me how these heaven-sent woes came rushing on the house; say how the children met their sad mischance.

MESSENGER Victims to purify the house were stationed before the altar of Zeus, for Heracles had slain and cast from his halls the king of the land. There stood his group of lovely children, with his sire and Megara; and already the basket was being passed round the altar, and we were keeping holy silence. But just as Alcmena's son was bringing the torch in his right hand to dip it in the holy water, he stopped without a word. And as their father lingered, his children looked at him; and lo! he was changed; his eyes were rolling; he was distraught; his eyeballs were bloodshot and starting from their sockets, and foam was oozing down his bearded cheek. Anon he spoke, laughing the while a madman's laugh, "Father, why should I sacrifice before I have slain Eurystheus, why kindle the purifying flame and have the toil twice over, when I might at one stroke so fairly end it all? Soon as I have brought the head of Eurystheus hither, I will cleanse my hands for those already slain. Spill the water, cast the baskets from your hands. Ho! give me now my bow and club! To famed Mycenae will I go; crow-bars and pick-axes must I take, for I will heave from their very base with iron levers those city-walls which the Cyclopes squared with red plumb-line and mason's tools."

Then he set out, and though he had no chariot there, he thought he had, and was for mounting to its seat, and using a goad as though his fingers really held one. A twofold feeling filled his servants' breasts, half amusement, and half fear; and one looking to his neighbour said, "Is our master making sport for us, or is he mad?" But he the while was pacing to and fro in his house; and, rushing into the men's chamber, he thought he had reached the city of Nisus, albeit he had gone into his own halls. So he threw himself upon the floor, as if he were there, and made ready to feast. But after waiting a brief space he began saying he was on his way to the plains amid the valleys of the Isthmus; and then stripping himself of his mantle, he fell to competing with an imaginary rival, o'er whom he proclaimed himself victor with his own voice, calling on imaginary spectators to listen. Next, fancy carrying him to Mycenae, he was uttering fearful threats against Eurystheus. Meantime his father caught him by his stalwart arm, and thus addressed him, "My son, what meanest thou hereby? What strange doings are these? Can it be that the blood of thy late victims has driven thee frantic?" But he, supposing it was the father of Eurystheus striving in abject supplication to touch his hand, thrust him aside, and then against his own children aimed his bow and made ready his quiver, thinking to slay the sons of Eurystheus. And they in wild affright darted hither and thither, one to his hapless mother's skirts, another to the shadow of a pillar, while a third cowered 'neath the altar like a bird. Then cried their mother, "O father, what art thou doing? dost mean to slay thy children?" Likewise his aged sire and all the gathered servants cried aloud. But he, hunting the child round and round, the column, in dreadful circles, and coming face to face with him shot him to the heart; and he fell upon his back, sprinkling the stone pillars with blood as he gasped out his life. Then did Heracles shout for joy and boasted loud, "Here lies one of Eurystheus' brood dead at my feet, atoning for his father's hate." Against a second did he aim his bow, who had crouched at the altar's foot thinking to escape unseen. But ere he fired, the poor child threw himself at his father's knees, and, flinging his hand to reach his beard or neck, cried, "Oh! slay me not, dear father mine! I am thy child, thine own; 'tis no son of Eurystheus thou wilt slay."

But that other, with savage Gorgon-scowl, as the child now stood in range of his baleful archery, smote him on the head, as smites a smith his molten iron, bringing down his club upon the fair-haired boy, and crushed the bones. The second caught, away he hies to add a third victim to the other twain. But ere he could, the poor mother caught up her babe and carried him within the house and shut the doors; forthwith the madman, as though he really were at the Cyclopean walls, prizes open the doors with levers, and, hurling down their posts, with one fell shaft laid low his wife and child. Then in wild career he starts to slay his aged sire; but lo! there came a phantom,-so it seemed to us on-lookers,-Of Pallas, with plumed helm, brandishing a spear; and she hurled a rock against the breast of Heracles, which stayed him from his frenzied thirst for blood and plunged him into sleep; to the ground he fell, smiting his back against a column that had fallen on the floor in twain when the roof fell in. Thereon we rallied from our flight, and with the old man's aid bound him fast with knotted cords to the pillar, that on his awakening he might do no further evil. So there he sleeps, poor wretch! a sleep that is not blest, having murdered wife and children; nay, for my part know not any son of man more miserable than he. (The MESSENGER withdraws.)

CHORUS (singing) That murder wrought by the daughters of Danaus, whereof my native Argos wots, was formerly the most famous and notorious in Hellas; but this hath surpassed and outdone those previous horrors. I could tell of the murder of that poor son of Zeus, whom Procne, mother of an only child, slew and offered to the Muses; but thou hadst three children, wretched parent, and all of them hast thou in thy frenzy slain. What groans or wails, what funeral dirge, or chant of death am I to raise? Alas and woe! see, the bolted doors of the lofty palace are being rolled apart. Ah me! behold these children lying dead before their wretched father, who is sunk in awful slumber after shedding their blood. Round him are bonds and cords, made fast with many a knot about the body of Heracles, and lashed to the stone columns of his house. While he, the aged sire, like mother-bird wailing her unfledged brood, comes hasting hither with halting steps on his bitter journey. (The central doors of the palace have opened and have disclosed HERACLES lying asleep, bound to a shattered column. AMPHITRYON steps out. The following lines between AMPHITRYON and the CHORUS are chanted responsively.)

AMPHITRYON Softly, softly! ye aged sons of Thebes, let him sleep on and forget his sorrows.

CHORUS For thee, old friend, I weep and mourn, for the children too and that victorious chief.

AMPHITRYON Stand further off, make no noise nor outcry, rouse him not from his calm deep slumber.

CHORUS O horrible! all this blood-

AMPHITRYON Hush, hush! ye will be my ruin.

CHORUS That he has spilt is rising up against him.

AMPHITRYON Gently raise your dirge of woe, old friends; lest he wake, and, bursting his bonds, destroy the city, rend his sire, and dash his house to pieces.

CHORUS I cannot, cannot-

AMPHITRYON Hush! let me note his breathing; come, let me put my ear close.

CHORUS Is he sleeping?

AMPHITRYON Aye, that is he, a deathly sleep, having slain wife and children with the arrows of his twanging bow.

CHORUS Ah! mourn-

AMPHITRYON I do.

CHORUS The children's death;

AMPHITRYON Ah me!

CHORUS And thy own son's doom.

AMPHITRYON Ah misery!

CHORUS Old friend-

AMPHITRYON Hush! hush! he is turning, he is waking! Oh Oh! let me hide myself beneath the covert of yon roof.

CHORUS Courage! darkness still broods o'er thy son's eye.

AMPHITRYON Oh! beware; 'tis not that I shrink from leaving the light after my miseries, poor wretch! but should he slay me that am his father, then will he be devising woe on woe, and to the avenging curse will add a parent's blood.

CHORUS Well for thee hadst thou died in that day, when, to win thy wife, thou didst go forth to exact vengeance for her slain brethren by sacking the Taphians' sea-beat town.

AMPHITRYON Fly, fly, my aged friends, haste from before the palace, escape his waking fury! For soon will he heap up fresh carnage on the old, ranging wildly once more through the streets of Thebes.

CHORUS O Zeus, why hast thou shown such savage hate against thine own son and plunged him in this sea of troubles?

HERACLES (waking) Aha! my breath returns; I am alive; and my eyes see, opening on the sky and earth and yon sun's darting beam; but how my senses reel! in what strange turmoil am I plunged! my fevered breath in quick spasmodic gasps escapes my lungs. How now? why am I lying here, made fast with cables like a ship, my brawny chest and arms tied to a shattered piece of masonry, with corpses for my neighbours; while o'er the floor my bow and arrows are scattered, that erst like trusty squires to my arm both kept me safe and were kept safe of me? Surely I am not come a second time to Hades' halls, having just returned from thence for Eurystheus? No, I do not see Sisyphus with his stone, or Pluto, or his queen, Demeter's child. Surely I am distraught; I cannot remember where I am. Ho, there! which of my friends is near or far to help me in my ignorance? For I have no clear knowledge of things once familiar.

AMPHITRYON My aged friends, shall I approach the scene of my sorrow?

LEADER OF THE CHORUS Yes, and let me go with thee, nor desert thee in thy trouble.

HERACLES Father, why dost thou weep and veil thy eyes, standing aloof from thy beloved son?

AMPHITRYON My child! mine still, for all thy misery.

HERACLES Why, what is there so sad in my case that thou dost weep?

AMPHITRYON That which might make any of the gods weep, were he to suffer so.

HERACLES A bold assertion that, but thou art not yet explaining what has happened.

AMPHITRYON Thine own eyes see that, if by this time thou are restored to thy senses.

HERACLES Fill in thy sketch if any change awaits my life.

AMPHITRYON I will explain, if thou art no longer mad as a fiend of hell.

HERACLES God help us! what suspicions these dark hints of thine again excite!

AMPHITRYON I am still doubtful whether thou art in thy sober senses.

HERACLES I never remember being mad.

AMPHITRYON Am I to loose my son, old friends, or

what?

HERACLES Loose and say who bound me; for I feel shame at this.

AMPHITRYON Rest content with what thou knowest of thy woes; the rest forego.

HERACLES Enough! I have no wish to probe thy silence.

AMPHITRYON O Zeus, dost thou behold these deeds proceeding from the throne of Hera?

HERACLES What! have I suffered something from her enmity?

AMPHITRYON A truce to the goddess! attend to thy own troubles.

HERACLES I am undone; what mischance wilt thou unfold?

AMPHITRYON See here the corpses of thy children.

HERACLES O horror! what hideous sight is here? ah me!

AMPHITRYON My son, against thy children hast thou waged unnatural war.

HERACLES War! what meanst thou? who killed these?

AMPHITRYON Thou and thy bow and some god, whoso he be that is to blame.

HERACLES What sayst thou? what have I done? Speak, father, thou messenger of evil.

AMPHITRYON Thou wert distraught; 'tis a sad explanation thou art asking.

HERACLES Was it I that slew my wife also?

AMPHITRYON Thy own unaided arm hath done all this.

HERACLES Ah, woe is me! a cloud of sorrow wraps me round.

AMPHITRYON The reason this that I lament thy fate.

HERACLES Did I dash my house to pieces or incite others thereto?

AMPHITRYON Naught know I save this, that thou art utterly undone.

HERACLES Where did my frenzy seize me? where did it destroy me?

AMPHITRYON In the moment thou wert purifying thyself witb fire at the altar.

HERACLES Ah me! why do I spare my own life when I have taken that of my dear children? Shall I not hasten to leap from some sheer rock, or aim the sword against my heart and avenge my children's blood, or burn my body in the fire and so avert from my life the infamy which now awaits me?

But hither I see Theseus coming to check my deadly counsels, my kinsman and friend. Now shall I stand revealed, and the dearest of my friends will see the pollution I have incurred by my children's murder. Ah, woe is me! what am I to do? Where can I find release from my sorrows? shall I take wings or plunge beneath the earth? Come, let me veil my head in darkness; for I am ashamed of the evil I have done, and, since for these I have incurred fresh blood-guiltiness, I would fain not harm the innocent. (THESEUS and his retinue enter.)

THESEUS I am come, and others with me, young warriors from the land of Athens, encamped by the streams of Asopus, to help thy son, old friend. For a rumour reached the city of the Erechtheidae, that Lycus had usurped the sceptre of this land and was become your enemy even to battle. Wherefore I came making recompense for the former kindness of Heracles in saving me from the world below, if haply ye have any need of such aid as I or my allies can give, old prince.

Ha! what means this heap of dead upon the floor? Surely I have not delayed too long and come too late to check new ills? Who slew these children? whose wife is this I see? Boys do not go to battle; nay, it must be some other strange mischance I here discover. (The following lines between THESEUS and AMPHITRYON are chanted responsively.)

AMPHITRYON O king, whose home is that olive-clad hill!

THESEUS Why this piteous prelude in addressing me?

AMPHITRYON Heaven has afflicted us with grievous suffering.

THESEUS Whose be these children, o'er whom thou weepest?

AMPHITRYON My own son's children, woe to him! their father and butcher both was he, hardening his heart to the bloody deed.

THESEUS Hush good words only!

AMPHITRYON I would I could obey!

THESEUS What dreadful words!

AMPHITRYON Fortune has spread her wings, and we are ruined, ruined.

THESEUS What meanest thou? what hath he done?

AMPHITRYON Slain them in a wild fit of frenzy with arrows dipped in the venom of the hundred-headed hydra.

THESEUS This is Hera's work; but who lies there among the dead, old man?

AMPHITRYON My son, my own enduring son, that marched with gods to Phlegra's plain, there to battle with giants and slay them, warrior that he was.

THESEUS Ah, woe for him! whose fortune was e'er so curst as his?

AMPHITRYON Never wilt thou find another that hath borne a larger share of suffering or been more fatally deceived.

THESEUS Why doth he veil his head, poor wretch, in his robe?

AMPHITRYON He is ashamed to meet thine eye; his kinsman's kind intent and his children's blood make him abashed.

THESEUS But I come to sympathize; uncover him.

AMPHITRYON My son, remove that mantle from thine eyes, throw it from thee, show thy fare unto the sun; a counterpoise to weeping is battling for the mastery. In suppliant wise I entreat thee, as I grasp thy beard, thy knees, thy hands, and let fall the tear from my old eyes. O my child! restrain thy savage lion-like temper, for thou art rushing forth on an unholy course of bloodshed, eager to join woe to woe.

THESEUS Ho! To thee I call who art huddled there in thy misery, show to they friends thy face; for no darkness is black enough to hide thy sad mischance. Why dost thou wave thy hand at me, signifying murder? is it that I may not be polluted by speaking with thee? If I share thy misfortune, what is that to me? For if I too had luck in days gone by, must refer it to the time when thou didst bring me safe from the dead to the light of life. I hate a friend whose gratitude grows old; one who ready to enjoy his friends' prosperity but unwilling to sail in the same ship with them when their fortune lours. Arise, unveil thy head, poor wretch! and look on me. The gallant soul endures without a word such blows as heaven deals.

HERACLES O Theseus, didst thou witness this struggle with my children?

THESEUS I heard of it, and now I see the horrors thou meanest.

HERACLES Why then hast thou unveiled my head to the sun?

THESEUS Why have I? Thou, a man, canst not pollute what is of God.

HERACLES Fly, luckless wretch, from my unholy taint.

THESEUS The avenging fiend goes not forth from friend to friend.

HERACLES For this I thank thee; I do not regret the service I did thee.

THESEUS While I, for kindness then received, now show my pity for thee.

HERACLES Ah yes! I am piteous, a murderer of my sons.

THESEUS I weep for thee in thy changed fortunes.

HERACLES Didst ever find another more afflicted?

THESEUS Thy misfortunes reach from earth to heaven.

HERACLES Therefore am I resolved on death.

THESEUS Dost thou suppose the gods attend to these thy threats?

HERACLES Remorseless hath heaven been to me; so I will prove the like to it.

THESEUS Hush! lest thy presumption add to thy sufferings.

HERACLES My barque is freighted full with sorrow; there is no room to stow aught further.

THESEUS What wilt thou do? whither is thy fury drifting thee?

HERACLES I will die and return to that world below whence I have just come.

THESEUS Such language is fit for any common fellow.

HERACLES Ah! thine is the advice of one outside sorrow's pale.

THESEUS Are these indeed the words of Heracles, the much-enduring?

HERACLES Though never so much as this. Endurance must have a limit.

THESEUS Is this man's benefactor, his chiefest friend?

HERACLES Man brings no help to me; no! Hera has her way.

THESEUS Never will Hellas suffer thee to die through sheer perversity.

HERACLES Hear me a moment, that I may enter the lists with words in answer to thy admonitions; and I will unfold to thee why life now as well as formerly has been unbearable to me. First I am the son of a man who incurred the guilt of blood, before he married my mother Alcmena, by slaying her aged sire. Now when the foundation is badly laid at birth, needs must the race be cursed with woe; and Zeus, whoever this Zeus may be, begot me as a butt for Hera's hate; yet be not thou vexed thereat, old man; for thee rather than Zeus do I regard as my father. Then whilst I was yet being suckled, that bride of Zeus did foist into my cradle fearsome snakes to compass my death. After I was grown to man's estate, of all the toils I then endured what need to tell? of all the lions, Typhons triple-bodied, and giants that I slew; or of the battle I won against the hosts of four-legged Centaurs? or how when I had killed the hydra, that monster with a ring of heads with power to grow again, I passed through countless other toils besides and came unto the dead to fetch to the light at the bidding of Eurystheus the three-headed hound, hell's porter. Last, ah, woe is me have I perpetrated this bloody deed to crown the sorrows of my house with my children's murder. To this sore strait am I come; no longer may I dwell in Thebes, the city that I love; for suppose I stay, to what temple or gathering of friends shall I repair? For mine is no curse that invites address. Shall I to Argos? how can I, when I am an exile from my country? Well, is there a single other city I can fly to? And if there were, am I to be looked at askance as a marked man, branded by cruel stabbing tongues, "Is not this the son of Zeus that once murdered wife and children? Plague take him from the land!"

Now to one who was erst called happy, such changes are a grievous thing; though he who is always unfortunate feels no such pain, for sorrow is his birthright. This, methinks, is the piteous pass I shall one day come to; for earth will cry out forbidding me to touch her, the sea and the river-springs will refuse me a crossing, and I shall become like Ixion who revolves in chains upon that wheel. Wherefore this is best, that henceforth I be seen by none of the Hellenes, amongst whom in happier days I lived in bliss. What right have I to live? what profit can I have in the possession of a useless, impious life? So let that noble wife of Zeus break forth in dancing, beating with buskined foot on heaven's bright floor; for now hath she worked her heart's desire in utterly confounding the chiefest of Hellas' sons. Who would pray to such a goddess? Her jealousy of Zeus for his love of a woman hath destroyed the benefactors of Hellas, guiltless though they were.

LEADER OF THE CHORUS This is the work of none other of the gods than the wife of Zeus; thou art right in that surmise.

THESEUS I cannot counsel you to die rather than to go on suffering. There is not a man alive that hath wholly 'scaped misfortune's taint, nor any god either, if what poets sing is true. Have they not intermarried in ways that law forbids? Have they not thrown fathers into ignominious chains to gain the sovereign power? Still they inhabit Olympus and brave the issue of their crimes. And yet what shalt thou say in thy defence, if thou, child of man, dost kick against the pricks of fate, while they do not? Nay, then, leave Thebes in compliance with the law, and come with me to the city of Pallas. There, when I have purified thee of thy pollution, will I give thee temples and the half of all I have. Yea, I will give thee all those presents I received from the citizens for saving their children, seven sons and daughters seven, on the day I slew the bull of Crete; for I have plots of land assigned me throughout the country; these shall henceforth be called after thee by men, whilst thou livest; and at thy death, when thou art gone to Hades' halls, the city of Athens shall unite in exalting thy honour with sacrifices and a monument of stone. For 'tis a noble crown for citizens to win from Hellas, even a reputation fair, by helping a man of worth. This is the return that I will make thee for saving me, for now art thou in need of friends. But when heaven delights to honour a man, he has no need of friends; for the god's aid, when he chooses to give it, is enough.

HERACLES Alas! this is quite beside the question of my troubles. For my part, I do not believe that the gods indulge in unholy unions; and as for putting fetters on parents' hands, I have never thought that worthy of belief, nor will I now be so persuaded, nor again that one god is naturally lord and master of another. For the deity, if he be really such, has no wants; these are miserable fictions of the poets. But I, for all my piteous plight, reflected whether I should let myself be branded as a coward for giving up my life. For whoso schooleth not his frail mortal nature to bear fate's buffets as he ought, will never be able to withstand even a man's weapon. I will harden my heart against death and seek thy city, with grateful thanks for all thou offerest me. (He weeps.) Of countless troubles have I tasted, God knows, but never yet did faint at any or shed a single tear; nay, nor ever dreamt that I should come to this, to let the tear-drop fall. But now, it seems, I must be fortune's slave. Well, let it pass; old father mine, thou seest me go forth to exile, and in me beholdest my own children's murderer. Give them burial and lay them out in death with the tribute of a tear, for the law forbids my doing so. Rest their heads upon their mother's bosom and fold them in her arms, sad pledges of our union, whom I, alas! unwittingly did slay. And when thou hast buried these dead, live on here still, in bitternes maybe, but still constrain thy soul to share my sorrows. O children! he who begat you, your own father, hath been your destroyer, and ye have had no profit of my triumphs, all my restless toil to win you a fair name in life, a glorious guerdon from a sire. Thee too, unhappy wife, this hand hath slain, a poor return to make thee for preserving mine honour so safe, for all the weary watch thou long hast kept within my house. Alas for you, my wife, my sons! and woe for me, how sad my lot, cut off from wife and child! Ah! these kisses, bitter-sweet! these weapons which 'tis pain to own! I am not sure whether to keep or let them go; dangling at my side they thus will say, "With us didst thou destroy children and wife; we are thy children's slayers, and thou keepest us." Shall I carry them after that? what answer can I make? Yet, am I to strip me of these weapons, the comrades of my glorious career in Hellas, and put myself thereby in the power of my foes, to die a death of shame? No! I must not let them go, but keep them, though it grieve me. In one thing, Theseus, help my misery; come to Argos with me and aid in settling my reward for bringing Cerberus thither; lest, if I go all alone, my sorrow for my sons do me some hurt.

O land of Cadmus, and all ye folk of Thebes! cut off your hair, and mourn with me; go to my children's burial, and with united dirge lament alike the dead and me; for on all of us hath Hera inflicted the same cruel blow of destruction.

THESEUS Rise, unhappy man! thou hast had thy fill of tears.

HERACLES I cannot rise; my limbs are rooted here.

THESEUS Yea, even the strong are o'erthrown by misfortunes.

HERACLES Ah! would I could grow into a stone upon this spot, oblivious of trouble!

THESEUS Peace! give thy hand to a friend and helper.

HERACLES Nay, let me not wipe off the blood upon thy robe.

THESEUS Wipe it off and spare not; I will not say thee nay.

HERACLES Reft of my own sons, I find thee as a son to me.

THESEUS Throw thy arm about my neck; I will be thy guide.

HERACLES A pair of friends in sooth are we, but one a man of sorrows. Ah! aged sire, this is the kind of man to make a friend.

AMPHITRYON Blest in her sons, the country that gave him birth!

HERACLES O Theseus, turn me back again to see my babes.

THESEUS What charm dost think to find in this to soothe thy soul?

HERACLES I long to do so, and would fain embrace my sire.

AMPHITRYON Here am I, my son; thy wish is no less dear to me.

THESEUS Hast thou so short a memory for thy troubles?

HERACLES All that I endured of yore was easier to bear than this.

THESEUS If men see thee play the woman, they will scoff.

HERACLES Have I by living grown so abject in thy sight? ‘twas not so once, methinks.

THESEUS Aye, too much so; for how dost show thyself the glorious Heracles of yore?

HERACLES What about thyself? what kind of hero wert thou when in trouble in the world below?

THESEUS I was worse than anyone as far as courage went.

HERACLES How then canst thou say of me, that I am abased by my troubles?

THESEUS Forward!

HERACLES Farewell, my aged sire!

AMPHITRYON Farewell to thee, my son!

HERACLES Bury my children as I said.

AMPHITRYON But who will bury me, my son?

HERACLES I will.

AMPHITRYON When wilt thou come?

HERACLES After thou hast buried my children.

AMPHITRYON How?

HERACLES I will fetch thee from Thebes to Athens. But carry my children within, a grievous burden to the earth. And I, after ruining my house by deeds of shame, will follow in the wake of Theseus, totally destroyed. Whoso prefers wealth or might to the possession of good friends, thinketh amiss. (THESEUS and his attendants lead HERACLES away.)

CHORUS (chanting) With grief and many a bitter tear we go our way, robbed of all we prized most dearly.

THE END

The Bacchae

Dramatis Personae

Dionysus
Cadmus
Pentheus
Agave
Teiresias
First Messenger
Second Messenger
Servant

Before the Palace of Pentheus at Thebes. Enter DIONYSUS.

DIONYSUS Lo! I am come to this land of Thebes, Dionysus' the son of Zeus, of whom on a day Semele, the daughter of Cadmus, was delivered by a flash of lightning. I have put off the god and taken human shape, and so present myself at Dirce's springs and the waters of Ismenus. Yonder I see my mother's monument where the bolt slew her nigh her house, and there are the ruins of her home smouldering with the heavenly flame that blazeth still-Hera's deathless outrage on my mother. To Cadmus all praise I offer, because he keeps this spot hallowed, his daughter's precinct, which my own hands have shaded round about with the vine's clustering foliage.

Lydia's glebes, where gold abounds, and Phrygia have I

left behind; o'er Persia's sun-baked plains, by Bactria's walled towns and Media's wintry clime have I advanced through Arabia, land of promise; and Asia's length and breadth, outstretched along the brackish sea, with many a fair walled town, peopled with mingled race of Hellenes and barbarians; and this is the first city in Hellas I have reached. There too have I ordained dances and established my rites, that I might manifest my godhead to men; but Thebes is the first city in the land of Hellas that I have made ring with shouts of joy, girt in a fawn-skin, with a thyrsus, my ivy-bound spear, in my hand; since my mother's sisters, who least of all should have done it, denied that Dionysus was the son of Zeus, saying that Semele, when she became a mother by some mortal lover, tried to foist her sin on Zeus-a clever ruse of Cadmus, which, they boldly asserted, caused Zeus to slay her for the falsehood about the marriage. Wherefore these are they whom I have driven frenzied from their homes, and they are dwelling on the hills with mind distraught; and I have forced them to assume the dress worn in my orgies, and all the women-folk of Cadmus' stock have I driven raving from their homes, one and all alike; and there they sit upon the roofless rocks beneath the green pine-trees, mingling amongst the sons of Thebes. For this city must learn, however loth, seeing that it is not initiated in my Bacchic rites, and I must take up my mother's defence, by showing to mortals that the child she bore to Zeus is a deity. Now Cadmus gave his sceptre and its privileges to Pentheus, his daughter's child, who wages war 'gainst my divinity, thrusting me away from his drink-offerings, and making no mention of me in his prayers. Therefore will I prove to him and all the race of Cadmus that I am a god. And when I have set all in order here, I will pass hence to a fresh country, manifesting myself; but if the city of Thebes in fury takes up arms and seeks to drive my votaries from the mountain, I will meet them at the head of my frantic rout. This is why I have assumed a mortal form, and put off my godhead to take man's nature.

O ye who left Tmolus, the bulwark of Lydia, ye women, my revel rout! whom I brought from your foreign homes to be ever by my side and bear me company, uplift the cymbals native to your Phrygian home, that were by me and the great mother Rhea first devised, and march around the royal halls of Pentheus smiting them, that the city of Cadmus may see you; while I will seek Cithaeron's glens, there with my Bacchanals to join the dance. (Exit DIONYSUS., Enter CHORUS.)

CHORUS From Asia o'er the holy ridge of Tmolus hasten to a pleasant task, a toil that brings no weariness, for Bromius' sake, in honour of the Bacchic god. Who loiters in the road? who lingers 'neath the roof? Avaunt! I say, and let every lip be hushed in solemn silence; for I will raise a hymn to Dionysus, as custom aye ordains. O happy he! who to his joy is initiated in heavenly mysteries and leads a holy life, joining heart and soul in Bacchic revelry upon the hills, purified from every sin; observing the rites of Cybele, the mighty mother, and brandishing the thyrsus, with ivy-wreathed head, he worships Dionysus. Go forth, go forth, ye Bacchanals, bring home the Bromian god Dionysus, child of a god, from the mountains of Phrygia to the spacious streets of Hellas, bring home the Bromian god! whom on a day his mother in her sore travail brought forth untimely, yielding up her life beneath the lightning stroke of Zeus' winged bolt; but forthwith Zeus, the son of Cronos, found for him another womb wherein to rest, for he hid him in his thigh and fastened it with golden pins to conceal him from Hera. And when the Fates had fully formed the horned god, he brought him forth and crowned him with a coronal of snakes, whence it is the thyrsus-bearing Maenads hunt the snake to twine about their hair. O Thebes, nurse of Semele! crown thyself with ivy; burst forth, burst forth with blossoms fair of green convolvulus, and with the boughs of oak and pine join in the Bacchic revelry; dor;-thy coat of dappled fawn-skin, decking it with tufts of silvered hair; with reverent hand the sportive wand now wield. Anon shall the whole land be dancing, when Bromius leads his revellers to the hills, to the hills away! where wait him groups of maidens from loom and shuttle roused in frantic haste by Dionysus. O hidden cave of the Curetes! O hallowed haunts in Crete, that saw Zeus born, where Corybantes with crested helms devised for me in their grotto the rounded timbrel of ox-hide, mingling Bacchic minstrelsy with the shrill sweet accents of the Phrygian flute, a gift bestowed by them on mother Rhea, to add its crash of music to the Bacchantes' shouts of joy; but frantic satyrs won it from the mother-goddess for their own, and added it to their dances in festivals, which gladden the heart of Dionysus, each third recurrent year. Oh! happy that votary, when from the hurrying revel-rout he sinks to earth, in his holy robe of fawnskin, chasing the goat to drink its blood, a banquet sweet of flesh uncooked, as he hastes to Phrygia's or to Libya's hills; while in the van the Bromian god exults with cries of Evoe. With milk and wine and streams of luscious honey flows the earth, and Syrian incense smokes. While the Bacchante holding in his hand a blazing torch of pine uplifted on his wand waves it, as he speeds along, rousing wandering votaries, and as he waves it cries aloud with wanton tresses tossing in the breeze; and thus to crown the revelry, he raises loud his voice, "On, on, ye Bacchanals, pride of Tmolus with its rills of gold I to the sound of the booming drum, chanting in joyous strains the praises of your joyous god with Phrygian accents lifted high, what time the holy lute with sweet complaining note invites you to your hallowed sport, according well with feet that hurry wildly to the hills; like a colt that gambols at its mother's side in the pasture, with gladsome heart each Bacchante bounds along." (Enter TEIRESIAS.)

TEIRESIAS What loiterer at the gates will call Cadmus from the house, Agenor's son, who left the city of Sidon and founded here the town of Thebes? Go one of you, announce to him that Teiresias is seeking him; he knows himself the reason of my coming and the compact I and he have made in our old age to bind the thyrsus with leaves and don the fawnskin, crowning our heads the while with ivy-sprays. (Enter CADMUS.)

CADMUS Best of friends! I was in the house when I heard thy voice, wise as its owner. I come prepared, dressed in the livery of the god. For 'tis but right I should magnify with all my might my own daughter's son, Dionysus, who hath shown his godhead unto men. Where are we to join the dance? where plant the foot and shake the hoary head? Do thou, Teiresias, be my guide, age leading age, for thou art wise. Never shall I weary, night or day, of beating the earth with my thyrsus. What joy to forget our years?

TEIRESIAS Why, then thou art as I am. For I too am young again, and will essay the dance.

CADMUS We will drive then in our chariot to the hill.

TEIRESIAS Nay, thus would the god not have an equal honour paid.

CADMUS Well, I will lead thee, age leading age.

TEIRESIAS The god will guide us both thither without toil.

CADMUS Shall we alone of all the city dance in Bacchus' honour?

TEIRESIAS Yea, for we alone are wise, the rest are mad.

CADMUS We stay too long; come, take my hand.

TEIRESIAS There link thy hand in my firm grip.

CADMUS Mortal that I am, I scorn not the gods.

TEIRESIAS No subtleties do I indulge about the powers of heaven. The faith we inherited from our fathers, old as time itself, no reasoning shall cast down; no! though it were the subtlest invention of wits refined. Maybe some one will say, I have no respect for my grey hair in going to dance with ivy round my head; not so, for the god did not define whether old or young should dance, but from all alike he claims a universal homage, and scorns nice calculations in his worship.

CADMUS Teiresias, since thou art blind, I must prompt thee what to say. Pentheus is coming hither to the house in haste, Echion's son, to whom I resign the government. How scared he looks I what strange tidings will he tell? (Enter PENTHEUS.)

PENTHEUS I had left my kingdom for awhile, when tidings of strange mischief in this city reached me; I hear that our women-folk have left their homes on pretence of Bacchic rites, and on the wooded hills rush wildly to and fro, honouring in the dance this new god Dionysus, whoe'er he is; and in the midst of each revel-rout the brimming wine-bowl stands, and one by one they steal away to lonely spots to gratify their lust, pretending forsooth that they are Maenads bent on sacrifice, though it is Aphrodite they are placing before the Bacchic god. As many as I caught, my gaolers are keeping safe in the public prison fast bound; and all who are gone forth, will I chase from the hills, Ino and Agave too who bore me to Echion, and Actaeon's mother Autonoe. In fetters of iron will I bind them and soon put an end to these outrageous Bacchic rites. They say there came a stranger hither, a trickster and a sorcerer, from Lydia's land, with golden hair and perfumed locks, the flush of wine upon his face, and in his eyes each grace that Aphrodite gives; by day and night he lingers in our maidens' company on the plea of teaching Bacchic mysteries. Once let me catch him within these walls, and I will put an end to his thyrsus-beating and his waving of his tresses, for I will cut his head from his body. This is the fellow who says that Dionysus is a god, says that he was once stitched up in the thigh of Zeus-that child who with his mother was blasted by the lightning flash, because the woman falsely said her marriage was with Zeus. Is not this enough to deserve the awful penalty of hanging, this stranger's wanton insolence, whoe'er he be?

But lo! another marvel. I see Teiresias, our diviner, dressed in dappled fawn-skins, and my mother's father too, wildly waving the Bacchic wand; droll sight enough! Father, it grieves me to see you two old men so void of sense. Oh! shake that ivy from thee! Let fall the thyrsus from thy hand, my mother's sire! Was it thou, Teiresias, urged him on to this? Art bent on introducing this fellow as another new deity amongst men, that thou mayst then observe the fowls of the air and make a gain from fiery divination? Were it not that thy grey hairs protected thee, thou shouldst sit in chains amid the Bacchanals, for introducing knavish mysteries; for where the gladsome grape is found at women's feasts, I deny that their rites have any longer good results.

CHORUS What impiety! Hast thou no reverence, sir stranger, for the gods or for Cadmus who sowed the crop of earth-born warriors? Son of Echion as thou art, thou dost shame thy birth.

TEIRESIAS Whenso a man of wisdom finds a good topic for argument, it is no difficult matter to speak well; but thou, though possessing a glib tongue as if endowed with sense, art yet devoid thereof in all thou sayest. A headstrong man, if he have influence and a capacity for speaking, makes a bad citizen because he lacks sense. This new deity, whom thou deridest, will rise to power I cannot say how great, throughout Hellas. Two things there are, young prince, that hold first rank among men, the goddess Demeter, that is, the earth, calf her which name thou please; she it is that feedeth men with solid food; and as her counterpart came this god, the son of Semele, who discovered the juice of the grape and introduced it to mankind, stilling thereby each grief that mortals suffer from, soon as e'er they are filled with the juice of the vine; and sleep also he giveth, sleep that brings forgetfulness of daily ills, the sovereign charm for all our woe. God though he is, he serves all other gods for libations, so that through him mankind is blest. He it is whom thou dost mock, because he was sewn up in the thigh of Zeus. But I will show thee this fair mystery. When Zeus had snatched him from the lightning's blaze, and to Olympus borne the tender babe, Hera would have cast him forth from heaven, but Zeus, as such a god well might, devised a counterplot. He broke off a fragment of the ether which surrounds the world, and made thereof a hostage against Hera's bitterness, while he gave out Dionysus into other hands; hence, in time, men said that he was reared in the thigh of Zeus, having changed the word and invented a legend, because the god was once a hostage to the goddess Hera. This god too hath prophetic power, for there is no small prophecy inspired by Bacchic frenzy; for whenever the god in his full might enters the human frame, he makes his frantic votaries foretell the future. Likewise he hath some share in Ares' rights; for oft, or ever a weapon is touched, a panic seizes an army when it is marshalled in array; and this too is a frenzy sent by Dionysus. Yet shalt thou behold him e'en on Delphi's rocks leaping o'er the cloven height, torch in hand, waving and brandishing the branch by Bacchus loved, yea, and through the length and breadth of Hellas. Hearken to me, Pentheus; never boast that might alone doth sway the world, nor if thou think so, unsound as thy opinion is, credit thyself with any wisdom; but receive the god into thy realm, pour out libations, join the revel rout, and crown thy head. It is not Dionysus that will force chastity on women in their love; but this is what we should consider, whether chastity is part of their nature for good and all; for if it is, no really modest maid will ever fall 'mid Bacchic mysteries. Mark this: thou thyself art glad when thousands throng thy gates, and citizens extol the name of Pentheus; he too, I trow, delights in being honoured. Wherefore I and Cadmus, whom thou jeerest so, will wreath our brows with ivy and join the dance; pair of grey beards though we be, still must we take part therein; never will I for any words of thine fight against heaven. Most grievous is thy madness, nor canst thou find a charm to cure thee, albeit charms have caused thy malady.

CHORUS Old sir, thy words do not discredit Phoebus, and thou art wise in honouring Bromius, potent deity.

CADMUS My son, Teiresias hath given thee sound advice; dwell with us, but o'erstep not the threshold of custom; for now thou art soaring aloft, and thy wisdom is no wisdom. E'en though he be no god, as thou assertest, still say he is; be guilty of a splendid fraud, declaring him the son of Semele, that she may be thought the mother of a god, and we and all our race gain honour. Dost thou mark the awful fate of Actaeon? whom savage hounds of his own rearing rent in pieces in the meadows, because he boasted himself a better hunter than Artemis. Lest thy fate be the same, come let me crown thy head with ivy; join us in rendering homage to the god.

PENTHEUS Touch me not away to thy Bacchic rites thyself! never try to infect me with thy foolery! Vengeance will

I have on the fellow who teaches thee such senselessness. Away one of you without delay! seek yonder seat where he observes his birds, wrench it from its base with levers, turn it upside down, o'erthrowing it in utter confusion, and toss his garlands to the tempest's blast. For by so doing shall I wound him most deeply. Others of you range the city and hunt down this girl-faced stranger, who is introducing a new complaint amongst our women, and doing outrage to the marriage tie. And if haply ye catch him, bring him hither to me in chains, to be stoned to death, a bitter ending to his revelry in Thebes. (Exit PENTHEUS.)

TEIRESIAS Unhappy wretch! thou little knowest what thou art saying. Now art thou become a raving madman, even before unsound in mind. Let us away, Cadmus, and pray earnestly for him, spite of his savage temper, and likewise for the city, that the god inflict not a signal vengeance. Come, follow me with thy ivy-wreathed staff; try to support my tottering frame as I do thine, for it is unseemly that two old men should fall; but let that-pass. For we must serve the Bacchic god, the son of Zeus. Only, Cadmus, beware lest Pentheus' bring sorrow to thy house; it is not my prophetic art, but circumstances that lead me to say this; for the words of a fool are folly. (Exeunt CADMUS and TEIRESIAS.)

CHORUS O holiness, queen amongst the gods, sweeping on golden pinion o'er the earth! dost hear the words of Pentheus, dost hear his proud blaspheming Bromius, the son of Semele; first of all the blessed gods at every merry festival? His it is to rouse the revellers to dance, to laugh away dull care, and wake the flute, whene'er at banquets of the gods the luscious grape appears, or when the winecup in the feast sheds sleep on men who wear the ivy-spray. The end of all unbridled speech and lawless senselessness is misery; but the life of calm repose and the rule of reason abide unshaken and support the home; for far away in heaven though they dwell, the powers divine behold man's state. Sophistry is not wisdom, and to indulge in thoughts beyond man's ken is to shorten life; and if a man on such poor terms should aim too high, he may miss the pleasures in his reach. These, to my mind, are the ways of madmen and idiots. Oh! to make my way to Cyprus, isle of Aphrodite, where dwell the love-gods strong to soothe man's soul, or to Paphos, which that foreign river, never fed by rain, enriches with its hundred mouths! Oh! lead me, Bromian god, celestial guide of Bacchic pilgrims, to the hallowed slopes of Olympus, where Pierian Muses have their haunt most fair. There dwell the Graces; there is soft desire; there thy votaries may hold their revels freely. The joy of our god, the son of Zeus, is in banquets, his delight is in peace, that giver of riches and nurse divine of youth. Both to rich and poor alike hath he granted the delight of wine, that makes all pain to cease; hateful to him is every one who careth not to live the life of bliss, that lasts through days and nights of joy. True wisdom is to keep the heart and soul aloof from over-subtle wits. That which the less enlightened crowd approves and practises, will I accept. (Re-enter PENTHEUS. Enter SERVANT bringing DIONYSUS bound.)

SERVANT We are come, Pentheus, having hunted down this prey, for which thou didst send us forth; not in vain hath been our quest. We found our quarry tame; he did not fly from us, but yielded himself without a struggle; his cheek ne'er blanched, nor did his ruddy colour change, but with a smile he bade me bind and lead him away, and he waited, making my task an easy one. For very shame I said to him, "Against my will, sir stranger, do I lead thee hence, but Pentheus ordered it, who sent me hither." As for his votaries whom thou thyself didst check, seizing and binding them hand and foot in the public gaol, all these have loosed their bonds and fled into the meadows where they now are sporting, calling aloud on the Bromian god. Their chains fell off their feet of their own accord, and doors flew open without man's hand to help. Many a marvel hath this stranger brought with him to our city of Thebes; what yet remains must be thy care.

PENTHEUS Loose his hands; for now that I have him in the net he is scarce swift enough to elude me. So, sir stranger, thou art not ill-favoured from a woman's point of view, which was thy real object in coming to Thebes; thy hair is long because thou hast never been a wrestler, flowing right down thy cheeks most wantonly; thy skin is white to help thee gain thy end, not tanned by ray of sun, but kept within the shade, as thou goest in quest of love with beauty's bait. Come, tell me first of thy race.

DIONYSUS That needs no braggart's tongue, 'tis easily told; maybe thou knowest Tmolus by hearsay.

PENTHEUS I know it, the range that rings the city of Sardis round.

DIONYSUS Thence I come, Lydia is my native home.

PENTHEUS What makes thee bring these mysteries to Hellas?

DIONYSUS Dionysus, the son of Zeus, initiated me.

PENTHEUS Is there a Zeus in Lydia, who begets new gods?

DIONYSUS No, but Zeus who married Semele in Hellas.

PENTHEUS Was it by night or in the face of day that he constrained thee?

DIONYSUS 'Twas face to face he intrusted his mysteries to me.

PENTHEUS Pray, what special feature stamps thy rites?

DIONYSUS That is a secret to be hidden from the uninitiated.

PENTHEUS What profit bring they to their votaries?

DIONYSUS Thou must not be told, though 'tis well worth knowing.

PENTHEUS A pretty piece of trickery, to excite my curiosity!

DIONYSUS A man of godless life is an abomination to the rites of the god.

PENTHEUS Thou sayest thou didst see the god clearly; what was he like?

DIONYSUS What his fancy chose; I was not there to order this.

PENTHEUS Another clever twist and turn of thine, without a word of answer.

DIONYSUS He were a fool, methinks, who would utter wisdom to a fool.

PENTHEUS Hast thou come hither first with this deity?

DIONYSUS All foreigners already celebrate these mysteries with dances.

PENTHEUS The reason being, they are far behind Hellenes in wisdom.

DIONYSUS In this at least far in advance, though their customs differ.

PENTHEUS Is it by night or day thou performest these devotions?

DIONYSUS By night mostly; darkness lends solemnity.

PENTHEUS Calculated to entrap and corrupt women.

DIONYSUS Day too for that matter may discover shame.

PENTHEUS This vile quibbling settles thy punishment.

DIONYSUS Brutish ignorance and godlessness will settle thine.

PENTHEUS How bold our Bacchanal is growing! a very master in this wordy strife!

DIONYSUS Tell me what I am to suffer; what is the grievous doom thou wilt inflict upon me?

PENTHEUS First will I shear off thy dainty tresses.

DIONYSUS My locks are sacred; for the god I let them grow.

PENTHEUS Next surrender that thyrsus.

DIONYSUS Take it from me thyself; 'tis the wand of Dionysus I am bearing.

PENTHEUS In dungeon deep thy body will I guard.

DIONYSUS The god himself will set me free, whene'er I list.

PENTHEUS Perhaps he may, when thou standest amid thy Bacchanals and callest on his name.

DIONYSUS Even now he is near me and witnesses my treatment.

PENTHEUS Why, where is he? To my eyes he is invisible.

DIONYSUS He is by my side; thou art a godless man and therefore dost not see him.

PENTHEUS Seize him! the fellow scorns me and Thebes too.

DIONYSUS I bid you bind me not, reason addressing madness.

PENTHEUS But I say "bind!" with better right than thou.

DIONYSUS Thou hast no knowledge of the life thou art leading; thy very existence is now a mystery to thee.

PENTHEUS I am Pentheus, son of Agave and Echion.

DIONYSUS Well-named to be misfortune's mate!

PENTHEUS Avaunt! Ho! shut him up within the horses' stalls hard by, that for light he may have pitchy gloom. Do thy dancing there, and these women whom thou bringest with thee to share thy villainies I will either sell as slaves or make their hands cease from this noisy beating of drums, and set them to work at the loom as servants of my own.

DIONYSUS I will go; for that which fate forbids, can never befall me. For this thy mockery be sure Dionysus will exact a recompense of thee-even the god whose existence thou deniest; for thou art injuring him by haling me to prison. (Exit DIONYSUS, guarded, and PENTHEUS.)

CHORUS Hail to thee, Dirce, happy maid, daughter revered of Achelous! within thy founts thou didst receive in days gone by the babe of Zeus, what time his father caught him up into his thigh from out the deathless flame, while thus he cried: "Go rest, my Dithyrambus, there within thy father's womb; by this name, O Bacchic god, I now proclaim thee to Thebes." But thou, blest Dirce, thrustest me aside, when in thy midst I strive to hold my revels graced with crowns. Why dost thou scorn me? Why avoid me? By the clustered charm that Dionysus sheds o'er the vintage I vow there yet shall come a time when thou wilt turn thy thoughts to Bromius. What furious rage the earth-born race displays, even Pentheus sprung of a dragon of old, himself the son of earth-born Echion, a savage monster in his very mien, not made in human mould, but like some murderous giant pitted against heaven; for he means to bind me, the handmaid of Bromius, in cords forthwith, and e'en now he keeps my fellow-reveller pent within his palace, plunged in a gloomy dungeon. Dost thou mark this, O Dionysus, son of Zeus, thy prophets struggling 'gainst resistless might? Come, O king, brandishing thy golden thyrsus along the slopes of Olympus; restrain the pride of this bloodthirsty wretch! Oh! where in Nysa, haunt of beasts, or on the peaks of Corycus art thou, Dionysus, marshalling with thy wand the revellers? or haply in the thick forest depths of Olympus, where erst Orpheus with his lute gathered trees to his minstrelsy, and beasts that range the fields. Ah blest Pieria! Evius honours thee, to thee will he come with his Bacchic rites to lead the dance, and thither will he lead the circling Maenads, crossing the swift current of Axius and the Lydias, that giveth wealth and happiness to man, yea, and the father of rivers, which, as I have heard, enriches with his waters fair a land of steeds.

DIONYSUS (Within) What ho! my Bacchantes, ho! hear my call, oh! hear.

CHORUS Who art thou? what Evian cry is this that calls me? whence comes it?

DIONYSUS What ho! once more I call, I the son of Semele, the child of Zeus.

CHORUS II My master, O my master, hail!

CHORUS III Come to our revel-band, O Bromian god.

CHORUS IV Thou solid earth!

CHORUS Most awful shock!

CHORUS VI O horror! soon will the palace of Pentheus totter and fall.

CHORUS VII Dionysus is within this house.

CHORUS VIII Do homage to him.

CHORUS IX We do! I do!

CHORUS Did ye mark yon architrave of stone upon the columns start asunder?

CHORUS XI Within these walls the triumph-shout of Bromius himself will rise.

DIONYSUS Kindle the blazing torch with lightning's fire, abandon to the flames the halls of Pentheus.

CHORUS XII Ha! dost not see the flame, dost not clearly mark it at the sacred tomb of Semele, the lightning flame which long ago the hurler of the bolt left there?

CHORUS XIII Your trembling limbs prostrate, ye Maenads, low upon the ground.

CHORUS XIV Yea, for our king, the son of Zeus, is assailing and utterly confounding this house. (Enter DIONYSUS.)

DIONYSUS Are ye so stricken with terror that ye have fallen to the earth, O foreign dames? Ye saw then, it would seem, how the Bacchic god made Pentheus' halls to quake; but arise, be of good heart, compose your trembling limbs.

CHORUS O chiefest splendour of our gladsome Bacchic sport, with what joy I see thee in my loneliness!

DIONYSUS Were ye cast down when I was led into the house, to be plunged into the gloomy dungeons of Pentheus?

CHORUS Indeed I was. Who was to protect me, if thou shouldst meet with mishap? But how wert thou set free from the clutches of this godless wretch?

DIONYSUS My own hands worked out my own salvation, easily and without trouble.

CHORUS But did he not lash fast thy hands with cords?

DIONYSUS There too I mocked him; he thinks he bound me, whereas he never touched or caught hold of me, but fed himself on fancy. For at the stall, to which he brought me for a gaol, he found a bull, whose legs and hoofs he straightly tied, breathing out fury the while, the sweat trickling from his body, and he biting his lips; but I from near at hand sat calmly looking on. Meantime came the Bacchic god and made the house quake, and at his mother's tomb relit the fire; but Pentheus, seeing this, thought his palace was ablaze, and hither and thither he rushed, bidding his servants bring water; but all in vain was every servant's busy toil. Thereon he let this labour be awhile, and, thinking maybe that I had escaped, rushed into the palace with his murderous sword unsheathed. Then did Bromius-so at least it seemed to me; I only tell you what I thought-made a phantom in the hall, and he rushed after it in headlong haste, and stabbed the lustrous air, thinking he wounded me. Further the Bacchic god did other outrage to him; he dashed the building to the ground, and there it lies a mass of ruin, a sight to make him rue most bitterly my bonds. At last from sheer fatigue he dropped his sword and fell fainting; for he a mortal frail, dared to wage war upon a god; but I meantime quietly left the house and am come to you, with never a thought of Pentheus. But methinks he will soon appear before the house; at least there is a sound of steps within. What will he say, I wonder, after this? Well, be his fury never so great, I will lightly bear it; for 'tis a wise man's way to school his temper into due control. (Enter PENTHEUS.)

PENTHEUS Shamefully have I been treated; that stranger, whom but now I made so fast in prison, hath escaped me. Ha! there is the man! What means this? How didst thou come forth, to appear thus in front of my palace?

DIONYSUS Stay where thou art; and moderate thy fury.

PENTHEUS How is it thou hast escaped thy fetters and art at large?

DIONYSUS Did I not say, or didst thou not hear me, "There is one will loose me."

PENTHEUS Who was it? there is always something strange in what thou sayest.

DIONYSUS He who makes the clustering vine to grow for man.

PENTHEUS (I scorn him and his vines!)

DIONYSUS A fine taunt indeed thou hurlest here at Dionysus!

PENTHEUS (To his servants) Bar every tower that hems us in, I order you.

DIONYSUS What use? Cannot gods pass even over walls?

PENTHEUS How wise thou art, except where thy wisdom is needed!

DIONYSUS Where most 'tis needed, there am I most wise. But first listen to yonder messenger and hear what he says; he comes from the hills with tidings for thee; and I will await thy pleasure, nor seek to fly. (Enter MESSENGER.) Messenger. Pentheus, ruler of this realm of Thebes! I am come from Cithaeron, where the dazzling flakes of pure white snow ne'er cease to fall.

PENTHEUS What urgent news dost bring me?

MESSENGER I have seen, O king, those frantic Bacchanals, who darted in frenzy from this land with bare white feet, and I am come to tell thee and the city the wondrous deeds they do, deeds passing strange. But I fain would hear, whether I am freely to tell all I saw there, or shorten my story; for I fear thy hasty temper, sire, thy sudden bursts of wrath and more than princely rage.

PENTHEUS Say on, for thou shalt go unpunished by me in all respects; for to be angered with the upright is wrong. The direr thy tale about the Bacchantes, the heavier punishment will I inflict on this fellow who brought his secret arts amongst our women.

MESSENGER I was just driving the herds of kine to a ridge of the hill as I fed them, as the sun shot forth his rays and made the earth grow warm; when lo! I see three revel-bands of women; Autonoe was chief of one, thy mother Agave of the second, while Ino's was the third. There they lay asleep, all tired out; some were resting on branches of the pine, others had laid their heads in careless ease on oak-leaves piled upon the ground, observing all modesty; not, as thou sayest, seeking to gratify their lusts alone amid the woods, by wine and soft flute-music maddened.

Anon in their midst thy mother uprose and cried aloud to wake them from their sleep, when she heard the lowing of my horned kine. And up they started to their feet, brushing from their eyes sleep's quickening dew, a wondrous sight of grace and modesty, young and old and maidens yet unwed. First o'er their shoulders they let stream their hair; then all did gird their fawn-skins up, who hitherto had left the fastenings loose, girdling the dappled hides with snakes that licked their cheeks. Others fondled in their arms gazelles or savage whelps of wolves, and suckled them-young mothers these with babes at home, whose breasts were still full of milk; crowns they wore of ivy or of oak or blossoming convolvulus. And one took her thyrsus and struck it into the earth, and forth there gushed a limpid spring; and another plunged her wand into the lap of earth and there the god sent up a fount of wine; and all who wished for draughts of milk had but to scratch the soil with their finger-tips and there they had it in abundance, while from every ivy-wreathed staff sweet rills of honey trickled.

Hadst thou been there and seen this, thou wouldst have turned to pray to the god, whom now thou dost disparage. Anon we herdsmen and shepherds met to discuss their strange and wondrous doings; then one, who wandereth oft to town and hath a trick of speech, made harangue in the midst, "O ye who dwell upon the hallowed mountain-terraces! shall we chase Agave, mother of Pentheus, from her Bacchic rites, and thereby do our prince a service?" We liked his speech, and placed ourselves in hidden ambush among the leafy thickets; they at the appointed time began to wave the thyrsus for their Bacchic rites, calling on Iacchus, the Bromian god, the son of Zeus, in united chorus, and the whole mount and the wild creatures re-echoed their cry; all nature stirred as they rushed on. Now Agave chanced to come springing near me, so up I leapt from out my ambush where I lay concealed, meaning to seize her. But she cried out, "What ho! my nimble hounds, here are men upon our track; but follow me, ay, follow, with the thyrsus in your hand for weapon." Thereat we fled, to escape being torn in pieces by the Bacchantes; but they, with hands that bore no weapon of steel, attacked our cattle as they browsed. Then wouldst thou have seen Agave mastering some sleek lowing calf, while others rent the heifers limb from limb. Before thy eyes there would have been hurling of ribs and hoofs this way and that; and strips of flesh, all blood-bedabbled, dripped as they hung from the pine-branches. Wild bulls, that glared but now with rage along their horns, found themselves tripped up, dragged down to earth by countless maidens' hands. The flesh upon their limbs was stripped therefrom quicker than thou couldst have closed thy royal eye-lids. Then off they sped, like birds that skim the air, to the plains beneath the hills, which bear a fruitful harvest for Thebes beside the waters of Asopus; to Hysiae and Erythrae, hamlets 'neath Cithaeron's peak, with fell intent, swooping on everything and scattering all pellmell; and they would snatch children from their homes; but all that they placed upon their shoulders, abode there firmly without being tied, and fell not to the dusky earth, not even brass or iron; and on their hair they carried fire and it burnt them not; but the country-folk rushed to arms, furious at being pillaged by Bacchanals; whereon ensued, O king, this wondrous spectacle. For though the ironshod dart would draw no blood from them, they with the thyrsus, which they hurled, caused many a wound and put their foes to utter rout, women chasing men, by some god's intervention. Then they returned to the place whence they had started, even to the springs the god had made to spout for them; and there washed off the blood, while serpents with their tongues were licking clean each gout from their cheeks. Wherefore, my lord and master, receive this deity, whoe'er he be, within the city; for, great as he is in all else, I have likewise heard men say, 'twas he that gave the vine to man, sorrow's antidote. Take wine away and Cypris flies, and every other human joy is dead.

CHORUS Though I fear to speak my mind with freedom in the presence of my king, still must I utter this; Dionysus yields to no deity in might.

PENTHEUS Already, look you! the presumption of these Bacchantes is upon us, swift as fire, a sad disgrace in the eyes of all Hellas. No time for hesitation now! away to the Electra gate! order a muster of all my men-at-arms, of those that mount fleet steeds, of all who brandish light bucklers, of archers too that make the bowstring twang; for I will march against the Bacchanals. By Heaven I this passes all, if we are to be thus treated by women. (Exit MESSENGER.)

DIONYSUS Still obdurate, O Pentheus, after hearing my words! In spite of all the evil treatment I am enduring from thee, still I warn thee of the sin of bearing arms against a god, and bid thee cease; for Bromius will not endure thy driving his votaries from the mountains where they revel.

PENTHEUS A truce to thy preaching to me! thou hast escaped thy bonds, preserve thy liberty; else will I renew thy punishment.

DIONYSUS I would rather do him sacrifice than in a fury kick against the pricks; thou a mortal, he a god.

PENTHEUS Sacrifice! that will I, by setting afoot a wholesale slaughter of women 'mid Cithaeron's glens, as they deserve.

DIONYSUS Ye will all be put to flight-a shameful thing that they with the Bacchic thyrsus should rout your mail-clad warriors.

PENTHEUS I find this stranger a troublesome foe to encounter; doing or suffering he is alike irrepressible.

DIONYSUS Friend, there is still a way to compose this bitterness.

PENTHEUS Say how; am I to serve my own servants?

DIONYSUS I will bring the women hither without weapons.

PENTHEUS Ha! ha! this is some crafty scheme of thine against me.

DIONYSUS What kind of scheme, if by my craft I purpose to save thee?

PENTHEUS You have combined with them to form this plot, that your revels may on for ever.

DIONYSUS Nay, but this is the compact I made with the god; be sure of that.

PENTHEUS (Preparing to start forth) Bring forth my

arms. Not another word from thee!

DIONYSUS Ha! wouldst thou see them seated on the hills?

PENTHEUS Of all things, yes! I would give untold sums for that.

DIONYSUS Why this sudden, strong desire?

PENTHEUS 'Twill be a bitter sight, if I find them drunk with wine.

DIONYSUS And would that be a pleasant sight which will prove bitter to thee?

PENTHEUS Believe me, yes! beneath the fir-trees as I sit in silence.

DIONYSUS Nay, they will track thee, though thou come secretly.

PENTHEUS Well, I will go openly; thou wert right to say so.

DIONYSUS Am I to be thy guide? wilt thou essay the road?

PENTHEUS Lead on with all speed, I grudge thee all delay.

DIONYSUS Array thee then in robes of fine linen.

PENTHEUS Why so? Am I to enlist among women after being a man?

DIONYSUS They may kill thee, if thou show thy manhood there.

PENTHEUS Well said! Thou hast given me a taste of thy wit already.

DIONYSUS Dionysus schooled me in this lore.

PENTHEUS How am I to carry out thy wholesome advice?

DIONYSUS Myself will enter thy palace and robe thee.

PENTHEUS What is the robe to be? a woman's? Nay, I am ashamed.

DIONYSUS Thy eagerness to see the Maenads goes no further.

PENTHEUS But what dress dost say thou wilt robe me in?

DIONYSUS Upon thy head will I make thy hair grow long.

PENTHEUS Describe my costume further.

DIONYSUS Thou wilt wear a robe reaching to thy feet; and on thy head shall be a snood.

PENTHEUS Wilt add aught else to my attire?

DIONYSUS A thyrsus in thy hand, and a dappled fawn-skin.

PENTHEUS I can never put on woman's dress.

DIONYSUS Then wilt thou cause bloodshed by coming to blows with the Bacchanals.

PENTHEUS Thou art right. Best go spy upon them first.

DIONYSUS Well, e'en that is wiser than by evil means to follow evil ends.

PENTHEUS But how shall I pass through the city of the Cadmeans unseen?

DIONYSUS We will go by unfrequented paths. I will lead the way.

PENTHEUS Anything rather than that the Bacchantes should laugh at me.

DIONYSUS We will enter the palace and consider the proper steps.

PENTHEUS Thou hast my leave. I am all readiness. I will enter, prepared to set out either sword in hand or following thy advice. (Exit PENTHEUS.)

DIONYSUS Women! our prize is nearly in the net. Soon shall he reach the Bacchanals, and there pay forfeit with his life. O Dionysus! now 'tis thine to act, for thou art not far away; let us take vengeance on him. First drive him mad by fixing in his soul a wayward frenzy; for never, whilst his senses are his own, will he consent to don a woman's dress; but when his mind is gone astray he will put it on. And fain would I make him a laughing-stock to Thebes as he is led in woman's dress through the city, after those threats with which he menaced me before. But I will go to array Pentheus in those robes which he shall wear when he sets out for Hades' halls, a victim to his own mother's fury; so shall he recognize Dionysus, the son of Zeus, who proves himself at last a god most terrible, for all his gentleness to man. (Exit DIONYSUS.)

CHORUS Will this white foot e'er join the night-long dance? what time in Bacchic ecstasy I toss my neck to heaven's dewy breath, like a fawn, that gambols 'mid the meadow's green delights, when she hath escaped the fearful chase, clear of the watchers, o'er the woven nets; while the huntsman, with loud halloo, harks on his hounds' full cry, and she with laboured breath at lightning speed bounds o'er the level water-meadows, glad to be far from man amid the foliage of the bosky grove. What is true wisdom, or what fairer boon has heaven placed in mortals' reach, than to gain the mastery o'er a fallen foe? What is fair is dear for aye. Though slow be its advance, yet surely moves the power of the gods, correcting those mortal wights, that court a senseless pride, or, in the madness of their fancy, disregard the gods. Subtly they lie in wait, through the long march of time, and so hunt down the godless man. For it is never right in theory or in practice to o'erride the law of custom. This is a maxim cheaply bought: whatever comes of God, or in time's long annals, has grown into a law upon a natural basis, this is sovereign. What is true wisdom, or what fairer boon has heaven placed in mortals' reach, than to gain the mastery o'er a fallen foe? What is fair is dear for ave. Happy is he who hath escaped the wave from out the sea, and reached the haven; and happy he who hath triumphed o'er his troubles; though one surpasses another in wealth and power; yet there be myriad hopes for all the myriad minds; some end in happiness for man, and others come to naught; but him, whose life from day to day is blest, I deem a happy man. (Enter DIONYSUS.)

DIONYSUS Ho! Pentheus, thou that art so cager to see what is forbidden, and to show thy zeal in an unworthy cause, come forth before the palace, let me see thee clad as a woman in frenzied Bacchante's dress, to spy upon thy own mother and her company. (Enter PENTHEUS.) Yes, thou resemblest closely a daughter of Cadmus.

PENTHEUS Of a truth I seem to see two suns, and two towns of Thebes, our seven-gated city; and thou, methinks, art a bull going before to guide me, and on thy head a pair of horns have grown. Wert thou really once a brute beast? Thon hast at any rate the appearance of a bull.

DIONYSUS The god attends us, ungracious heretofore, but now our sworn friend; and now thine eyes behold the things they should.

PENTHEUS Pray, what do I resemble? Is not mine the carriage of Ino, or Agave my own mother?

DIONYSUS In seeing thee, I seem to see them in person. But this tress is straying from its place, no longer as I bound it 'neath the snood.

PENTHEUS I disarranged it from its place as I tossed it to and fro within my chamber, in Bacchic ecstasy.

DIONYSUS Well, I will rearrange it, since to tend thee is my care; hold up thy head.

PENTHEUS Come, put it straight; for on thee do I depend.

DIONYSUS Thy girdle is loose, and the folds of thy dress

do not hang evenly below thy ankles.

PENTHEUS I agree to that as regards the right side, but on the other my dress hangs straight with my foot.

DIONYSUS Surely thou wilt rank me first among thy friends, when contrary to thy expectation thou findest the Bacchantes virtuous.

PENTHEUS Shall I hold the thyrsus in the right or left hand to look most like a Bacchanal?

DIONYSUS Hold it in thy right hand, and step out with thy right foot; thy change of mind compels thy praise.

PENTHEUS Shall I be able to carry on my shoulders Cithaeron's glens, the Bacchanals and all?

DIONYSUS Yes, if so thou wilt; for though thy mind was erst diseased, 'tis now just as it should be.

PENTHEUS Shall we take levers, or with my hands can I uproot it, thrusting arm or shoulder 'neath its peaks?

DIONYSUS No, no! destroy not the seats of the Nymphs and the haunts of Pan, the place of his piping.

PENTHEUS Well said! Women must not be mastered by brute force; amid the pines will I conceal myself.

DIONYSUS Thou shalt hide thee in the place that fate appoints, coming by stealth to spy upon the Bacchanals.

PENTHEUS Why, methinks they are already caught in the pleasant snares of dalliance, like birds amid the brakes.

DIONYSUS Set out with watchful heed then for this very purpose; maybe thou wilt catch them, if thou be not first caught thyself.

PENTHEUS Conduct me through the very heart of Thebes, for I am the only man among them bold enough to do this deed.

DIONYSUS Thou alone bearest thy country's burden,

thou and none other; wherefore there await thee such struggles as needs must. Follow me, for I will guide thee safely thither; another shall bring thee thence.

PENTHEUS My mother maybe.

DIONYSUS For every eye to see.

PENTHEUS My very purpose in going.

DIONYSUS Thou shalt be carried back,

PENTHEUS What luxury

DIONYSUS In thy mother's arms.

PENTHEUS Thou wilt e'en force me into luxury.

DIONYSUS Yes, to luxury such as this.

PENTHEUS Truly, the task I am undertaking deserves it. (Exit PENTHEUS.)

DIONYSUS Strange, ah! strange is thy career, leading to scenes of woe so strange, that thou shalt achieve a fame that towers to heaven. Stretch forth thy hands, Agave, and ye her sisters, daughters of Cadmus; mighty is the strife to which I am bringing the youthful king, and the victory shall rest with me and Bromius; all else the event will show. (Exit DIONYSUS.)

CHORUS To the hills! to the hills! fleet hounds of madness, where the daughters of Cadmus hold their revels, goad them into wild fury against the man disguised in woman's dress, a frenzied spy upon the Maenads. First shall his mother mark him as he peers from some smooth rock or riven tree, and thus to the Maenads she will call, "Who is this of Cadmus' sons comes hasting to the mount, to the mountain away, to spy on us, my Bacchanals? Whose child can he be? For he was never born of woman's blood; but from some lioness maybe or Libyan Gorgon is he sprung." Let justice appear and show herself, sword in hand, to plunge it through and through the throat of the godless, lawless, impious son of Echion, earth's monstrous child! who with wicked heart and lawless rage, with mad intent and frantic purpose, sets out to meddle with thy holy rites, and with thy mother's, Bacchic god, thinking with his weak arm to master might as masterless as thine. This is the life that saves all pain, if a man confine his thoughts to human themes, as is his mortal nature, making no pretence where heaven is concerned. I envy not deep subtleties; far other joys have I, in tracking out great truths writ clear from all eternity, that a man should live his life by day and night in purity and holiness, striving toward a noble goal, and should honour the gods by casting from him each ordinance that lies outside the pale of right. Let justice show herself, advancing sword in hand to plunge it through and through the throat of Echion's son, that godless, lawless, and abandoned child of earth! Appear, O Bacchus, to our eyes as a bull or serpent with a hundred heads, or take the shape of a lion breathing flame! Oh! come, and with a mocking smile cast the deadly noose about the hunter of thy Bacchanals, e'en as he swoops upon the Maenads gathered yonder. (Enter SECOND MESSENGER.)

SECOND MESSENGER O house, so prosperous once through Hellas long ago, home of the old Sidonian prince, who sowed the serpent's crop of earth-born men, how do I mourn thee! slave though I be, yet still the sorrows of his master touch a good slave's heart.

CHORUS How now? Hast thou fresh tidings of the Bacchantes?

SECOND MESSENGER Pentheus, Echion's son is dead.

CHORUS Bromius, my king! now art thou appearing in thy might divine.

SECOND MESSENGER Ha! what is it thou sayest? art thou glad, woman, at my master's misfortunes?

CHORUS A stranger I, and in foreign tongue I express my joy, for now no more do I cower in terror of the chain.

SECOND MESSENGER Dost think Thebes so poor in men?(*, * Probably the whole of one iambic line with part of another is here lost.)

CHORUS 'Tis Dionysus, Dionysus, not Thebes that lords it over me.

SECOND MESSENGER All can I pardon thee save this; to exult o'er hopeless suffering is sorry conduct, dames.

CHORUS Tell me, oh! tell me how he died, that villain scheming villainy!

SECOND MESSENGER Soon as we had left the homesteads of this Theban land and had crossed the streams of Asopus, we began to breast Cithaeron's heights, Pentheus and I, for I went with my master, and the stranger too, who was to guide us to the scene. First then we sat us down in a grassy glen, carefully silencing each footfall and whispered breath, to see without being seen. Now there was a dell walled in by rocks, with rills to water it, and shady pines o'erhead; there were the Maenads seated, busied with joyous toils. Some were wreathing afresh the drooping thyrsus with curling ivy-sprays; others, like colts let loose from the carved chariot-yoke, were answering each other in hymns of Bacchic rapture. But Pentheus, son of sorrow, seeing not the women gathered there, exclaimed, "Sir stranger, from where I stand, I cannot clearly see the mock Bacchantes; but I will climb a hillock or a soaring pine whence to see clearly the shameful doings of the Bacchanals." Then and there I saw the stranger work a miracle; for catching a lofty fir-branch by the very end he drew it downward to the dusky earth, lower yet and ever lower; and like a bow it bent, or rounded wheel, whose curving circle grows complete, as chalk and line describe it; e'en so the stranger drew down the mountain-branch between his hands, bending it to earth, by more than human agency. And when he had seated Pentheus aloft on the pine branches, he let them slip through his hands gently, careful not to shake him from his seat. Up soared the branch straight into the air above, with my master perched thereon, seen by the Maenads better far than he saw them; for scarce was he beheld upon his lofty throne, when the stranger disappeared, while from the sky there came a voice, 'twould seem, by Dionysus uttered-

"Maidens, I bring the man who tried to mock you and me and my mystic rites; take vengeance on him." And as he spake he raised 'twixt heaven and earth a dazzling column of awful flame. Hushed grew the sky, and still hung each leaf throughout the grassy glen, nor couldst thou have heard one creature cry. But they, not sure of the voice they heard, sprang up and peered all round; then once again his bidding came; and when the daughters of Cadmus knew it was the Bacchic god in very truth that called, swift as doves they dirted off in cager haste, his mother Agave and her sisters dear and all the Bacchanals; through torrent glen, o'er boulders huge they bounded on, inspired with madness by the god. Soon as they saw my master perched upon the fir, they set to hurling stones at him with all their might, mounting a commanding eminence, and with pine-branches he was pelted as with darts; and others shot their wands through the air at Pentheus, their hapless target, but all to no purpose. For there he sat beyond the reach of their hot endeavours, a helpless, hopeless victim. At last they rent off limbs from oaks and were for prising up the roots with levers not of iron. But when they still could make no end to all their toil, Agave cried: "Come stand around, and grip the sapling trunk, my Bacchanals! that we may catch the beast that sits thereon, lest he divulge the secrets of our god's religion."

Then were a thousand hands laid on the fir, and from the ground they tore it up, while he from his seat aloft came tumbling to the ground with lamentations long and loud, e'en Pentheus; for well he knew his hour was come. His mother first, a priestess for the nonce, began the bloody deed and fell upon him; whereon he tore the snood from off his hair, that hapless Agave might recognize and spare him, crying as he touched her cheek, "O mother! it is I, thy own son Pentheus, the child thou didst bear in Echion's halls; have pity on me, mother dear! oh! do not for any sin of mine slay thy own son."

But she, the while, with foaming mouth and wildly rolling eyes, bereft of reason as she was, heeded him not; for the god possessed her. And she caught his left hand in her grip, and planting her foot upon her victim's trunk she tore the shoulder from its socket, not of her own strength, but the god made it an easy task to her hands; and Ino set to work upon the other side, rending the flesh with Autonoe and all the eager host of Bacchanals; and one united cry arose, the victim's groans while yet he breathed, and their triumphant shouts. One would make an arm her prey, another a foot with the sandal on it; and his ribs were stripped of flesh by their rending nails; and each one with blood-dabbled hands was tossing Pentheus' limbs about. Scattered lies his corpse, part beneath the rugged rocks, and part amid the deep dark woods, no easy task to find; but his poor head hath his mother made her own, and fixing it upon the point of a thyrsus, as it had been a mountain lion's, she bears it through the midst of Cithaeron, having left her sisters with the Maenads at their rites. And she is entering these walls exulting in her hunting fraught with woe, calling on the Bacchic god her fellow-hunter who had helped her to triumph in a chase, where her only prize was tears.

But I will get me hence, away from this piteous scene, before Agave reach the palace. To my mind self-restraint and reverence for the things of God point alike the best and wisest course for all mortals who pursue them. (Exit SECOND MESSENGER.)

CHORUS Come, let us exalt our Bacchic god in choral strain, let us loudly chant the fall of Pentheus from the serpent sprung, who assumed a woman's dress and took the fair Bacchic wand, sure pledge of death, with a bull to guide him to his doom. O ye Bacchanals of Thebes! glorious is the triumph ye have achieved, ending in sorrow and tears. 'Tis a noble enterprise to dabble the hand in the blood of a son till it drips. But hist! I see Agave, the mother of Pentheus, with wild rolling eye hasting to the house; welcome the revellers of the Bacchic god. (Enter AGAVE.)

AGAVE Ye Bacchanals from Asia

CHORUS Why dost thou rouse me? why?

AGAVE From the hills I am bringing to my home a tendril freshly-culled, glad guerdon-of the chase.

CHORUS I see it, and I will welcome thee unto our revels. All hail!

AGAVE I caught him with never a snare, this lion's whelp, as ye may see.

CHORUS From what desert lair?

AGAVE Cithaeron-

CHORUS Yes, Cithaeron?

AGAVE Was his death.

CHORUS Who was it gave the first blow?

AGAVE Mine that privilege; "Happy Agave!" they call me 'mid our revellers.

CHORUS Who did the rest?

AGAVE Cadmus-

CHORUS What of him?

AGAVE His daughters struck the monster after me; yes, after me.

CHORUS Fortune smiled upon thy hunting here.

AGAVE Come, share the banquet.

CHORUS Share? ah I what?

AGAVE 'Tis but a tender whelp, the down just sprouting on its cheek beneath a crest of failing hair.

CHORUS The hair is like some wild creature's.

AGAVE The Bacchic god, a hunter skilled, roused his Maenads to pursue this quarry skilfully.

CHORUS Yea, our king is a hunter indeed.

AGAVE Dost approve?

CHORUS Of course I do.

AGAVE Soon shall the race of Cadmus-

CHORUS And Pentheus, her own son, shall to his mother-

AGAVE Offer praise for this her quarry of the lion's brood.

CHORUS Quarry strange!

AGAVE And strangely caught.

CHORUS Dost thou exult?

AGAVE Right glad am I to have achieved a great and glorious triumph for my land that all can see.

CHORUS Alas for thee! show to the folk the booty thou hast won and art bringing hither.

AGAVE All ye who dwell in fair fenced Thebes, draw near that ye may see the fierce wild beast that we daughters of Cadmus made our prey, not with the thong-thrown darts of Thessaly, nor yet with snares, but with our fingers fair. Ought men idly to boast and get them armourers' weapons? when we with these our hands have caught this prey and torn the monster limb from limb? Where is my aged sire? let him approach. And where is Pentheus, my son? Let him bring a ladder and raise it against the house to nail up on the gables this lion's head, my booty from the chase. (Enter CADMUS.)

CADMUS Follow me, servants to the palace-front, with your sad burden in your arms, ay, follow, with the corpse of Pentheus, which after long weary search I found, as ye see it, torn to pieces amid Cithaeron's glens, and am bringing hither; no two pieces did I find together, as they lay scattered through the trackless wood. For I heard what awful deeds one of my daughters had done, just as I entered the city-walls with old Teiresias returning from the Bacchanals;

so I turned again unto the and bring from thence my son who was slain by Maenads. There I saw Autonoe, that bare Actaeon on a day to Aristaeus, and Ino with her, still ranging the oak-groves in their unhappy frenzy; but one told me that that Agave, was rushing wildly hither, nor was it idly said, for there I see her, sight of woe!

AGAVE Father, loudly mayst thou boast, that the daughters thou hast begotten are far the best of mortal race; of one and all I speak, though chiefly of myself, who left my shuttle at the loom for nobler enterprise, even to hunt savage beasts with my hands; and in my arms I bring my prize, as thou seest, that it may be nailed up on thy palace-wall; take it, father, in thy had and proud of my hunting, call thy friends to a banquet; for blest art thou, ah! doubly blest in these our gallant exploits.

CADMUS O grief that has no bounds, too cruel for mortal eye! 'tis murder ye have done with your hapless hands. Fair is the victim thou hast offered to the gods, inviting me and my Thebans to the feast Ah, woe is me first for thy sorrows, then for mine. What ruin the god, the Bromian king, hath brought on us, just maybe, but too severe, seeing he is our kinsman!

AGAVE How peevish old age makes men! what sullen looks! Oh, may my son follow in his mother's footsteps and be as lucky in his hunting, when he goes quest of game in company with Theban youthsl But he can do naught but wage war with gods. Father, 'tis thy duty to warn him. Who will summon him hither to my sight to witness my happiness?

CADMUS Alas for you! alas! Terrible will be your grief when ye are conscious of your deeds; could ye re. for ever till life's close in your present state, ye would not, spite of ruined bliss, appear so cursed with woe.

AGAVE Why? what is faulty bere? what here for sorrow?

CADMUS First let thine eye look up to heaven.

AGAVE See! I do so. Why dost thou suggest my looking thereupon?

CADMUS Is it still the same, or dost think there's any change?

AGAVE 'Tis brighter than it was, and dearer too.

CADMUS Is there still that wild unrest within thy soul?

AGAVE I know not what thou sayest now; yet methinks my brain is clearing, and my former frenzy passed away.

CADMUS Canst understand, and give distinct replies?

AGAVE Father, how completely I forget all we said before!

CADMUS To what house wert thou brought with marriage-hymns?

AGAVE Thou didst give me to earthborn Echion, as men call him.

CADMUS What child was born thy husband in his halls?

AGAVE Pentheus, of my union with his father.

CADMUS What head is that thou barest in thy arms?

AGAVE A lion's; at least they said so, who hunted it.

CADMUS Consider it aright; 'tis no great task to look at it.

AGAVE Ah! what do I see? what is this I am carrying in my hands?

CADMUS Look closely at it; make thy knowledge more certain.

AGAVE Ah, 'woe is me! O sight of awful sorrow!

CADMUS Dost think it like a lion's head?

AGAVE Ah no! 'tis Pentheus' head which I his unhappy

mother hold.

CADMUS Bemoaned by me, or ever thou didst recognize him.

AGAVE Who slew him? How came he into my hands?

CADMUS O piteous truth! how ill-timed thy presence here!

AGAVE Speak; my bosom throbs at this suspense.

CADMUS 'Twas thou didst slay him, thou and thy sisters.

AGAVE Where died he? in the house or where?

CADMUS On the very spot where hounds of yore rent Actaeon in pieces.

AGAVE Why went he, wretched youth! to Cithaeron?

CADMUS He would go and mock the god and thy Bacchic rites.

AGAVE But how was it we had journeyed thither?

CADMUS Ye were distraught; the whole city had the Bacchic frenzy.

AGAVE 'Twas Dionysus proved our ruin; now I see it all.

CADMUS Yes, for the slight he suffered; ye would not believe in his godhead.

AGAVE Father, where is my dear child's corpse?

CADMUS With toil I searched it out and am bringing it myself.

AGAVE Is it all fitted limb to limb in seemly wise? CADMUS (*, * One line, or maybe more, is missing)

AGAVE But what had Pentheus to do with folly of mine?

CADMUS He was like you in refusing homage to the god, who, therefore, hath involved you all in one common ruin, you and him alike, to destroy this house and me, forasmuch as I, that had no sons, behold this youth, the fruit of thy womb, unhappy mother! foully and most shamefully slain. To thee, my child, our house looked up, to thee my daughter's son, the stay of my palace, inspiring the city with awe; none caring to flout the old king when he saw thee by, for he would get his deserts. But now shall I be cast out dishonoured from my halls, Cadmus the great, who sowed the crop of Theban seed and reaped that goodly harvest. O beloved child! dead though thou art, thou still shalt be counted by me amongst my own dear children; no more wilt thou lay thy hand upon my chin in fond embrace, my child, and calling on thy mother's sire demand, "Who wrongs thee or dishonours thee, old sire? who vexes thy heart, a thorn within thy side? Speak, that I may punish thy oppressor, father mine!"

But now am I in sorrow plunged, and woe is thee, and woe thy mother and her suffering sisters too! Ah! if there be any man that scorns the gods, let him well mark this prince's death and then believe in them.

CHORUS Cadmus, I am sorry for thy fate; for though thy daughter's child hath met but his deserts, 'tis bitter grief to thee.

AGAVE O father, thou seest how sadly my fortune is changed.(*, * After this a very large lacuna occurs in the MS.)

DIONYSUS Thou shalt be changed into a serpent; and thy wife Harmonia, Ares' child, whom thou in thy human life didst wed, shall change her nature for a snake's, and take its form. With her shalt thou, as leader of barbarian tribes, drive thy team of steers, so saith an oracle of Zeus; and many a city shalt thou sack with an army numberless; but in the day they plunder the oracle of Loxias, shall they rue their homeward march; but thee and Harmonia will Ares rescue, and set thee to live henceforth in the land of the blessed. This do I declare, I Dionysus, son of no mortal father but of Zeus.

Had ye learnt wisdom when ye would not, ye would now be happy with the son of Zeus for your ally.

AGAVE O Dionysus! we have sinned; thy pardon we implore.

DIONYSUS Too late have ye learnt to know me; ye knew me not at the proper time.

AGAVE We recognize our error; but thou art too revengeful.

DIONYSUS Yea, for I, though a god, was slighted by you.

AGAVE Gods should not let their passion sink to man's level.

DIONYSUS Long ago my father Zeus ordained it thus.

AGAVE Alas! my aged sire, our doom is fixed; 'tis woful exile.

DIONYSUS Why then delay the inevitable? Exit.

CADMUS Daughter, to what an awful pass are we now come, thou too, poor child, and thy sisters, while I alas! in my old age must seek barbarian shores, to sojourn there; but the oracle declares that I shall yet lead an army, half-barbarian, half-Hellene, to Hellas; and in serpent's shape shall I carry my wife Harmonia, the daughter of Ares, transformed like me to a savage snake, against the altars and tombs of Hellas at the head of my troops; nor shall I ever cease from my woes, ah me! nor ever cross the downward stream of Acheron and be at rest.

AGAVE Father, I shall be parted from thee and exiled.

CADMUS Alas! my child, why fling thy arms around me, as a snowy cygnet folds its wings about the frail old swan?

AGAVE Whither can I turn, an exile from my country?

CADMUS I know not, my daughter; small help is thy father now.

AGAVE Farewell, my home! farewell, my native city! with sorrow I am leaving thee, an exile from my bridal bower.

CADMUS Go, daughter, to the house of Aristaeus,(*, * Another large lacuna follows.)

AGAVE Father, I mourn for thee.

CADMUS And I for thee, my child; for thy sisters too I shed a tear.

AGAVE Ah! terribly was king Dionysus bringing this outrage on thy house.

CADMUS Yea, for he suffered insults dire from you, his name receiving no meed of honour in Thebes.

AGAVE Farewell, father mine!

CADMUS Farewell, my hapless daughter and yet thou scarce canst reach that bourn.

AGAVE Oh! lead me, guide me to the place where I shall find my sisters, sharers in my exile to their sorrow! Oh! to reach a spot where cursed Cithaeron ne'er shall see me more nor I Cithaeron with mine eyes; where no memorial of the thyrsus is set up! Be they to other Bacchantes dear!

CHORUS Many are the forms the heavenly will assumes, and many a thing the gods fulfil contrary to all hope; that which was expected is not brought to pass, while for the unlooked-for Heaven finds out a way. E'en such hath been the issue here. (Exeunt OMNES.)

THE END

Made in the USA
Las Vegas, NV
25 July 2023

75227900R00095